SOCIAL CHANGE IN ISRAEL

POPULATION RESEARCH AND TRAINING CENTER MONOGRAPHS
UNIVERSITY OF CHICAGO

SOCIAL CHANGE IN ISRAEL

BY JUDAH MATRAS

ALDINE PUBLISHING COMPANY / CHICAGO

First published 1965 by
ALDINE Publishing Company
320 West Adams Street
Chicago, Illinois 60606

Library of Congress Catalog Card Number: 65-22491

Designed by David Miller
Printed in the United States of America

To Meyer Matras, teacher and grandfather

FOREWORD

Social Change in Israel makes a fresh and important contribution in several ways.

First, it marshalls and organizes data relating to Israel in a manner designed to complement the available literature and, hence, further illuminates the social structure and dynamics of this emergent nation. As a case study of one of the new political entities generated by World War II, this volume will be of interest to all concerned with new nations and the processes of nation-making. Moreover, the story of Israel is a widely heralded example of successful development and the material here presented can serve as a model for comparative study and analysis.

Second, Dr. Matras takes an important methodological step forward in combining widely used conceptual and theoretical frameworks of sociology with quantitative and empirical research methods. With great ingenuity he has wedded Talcott Parsons and S. F. Nadel with ecological and demographic techniques—no mean feat. Moreover, his skillful handling of both theory and method provides a test of the hypotheses developed by S. N. Eisenstadt regarding the absorption of immigrants and social change in Israel.

Third, the author is quite specific in indicating, on the one hand, what his goal is and, on the other, the extent to which he can only approximate it by reason of deficiencies in the available data. He thereby also makes a contribution in pointing to the ways in which demographic data should be improved to permit sharper and more refined analysis.

In addition to the novel general approach, the reader will find a number of specific methodological rewards, such as Dr.

Matras' analysis of "the strategy of family formation," his use of "ecological correlations" in his analysis of national parliamentary elections, and his handling of intergenerational occupational mobility.

This is the second in a new series of monographs prepared in the Population Research and Training Center of the University of Chicago. This volume had its origin in Dr. Judah Matras' Ph.D. dissertation in the Department of Sociology.

Dr. Matras served as Research Associate (Assistant Professor) in the Population Research and Training Center during the academic year 1963-64, on leave from his post at Hebrew University. As a member of the staff of the Center he not only pursued the research reported in this monograph but also engaged in other investigations of the strategy of family formation which will be the subject of further publications. It should be added that Dr. Matras during his year of residence as a member of the staff contributed significantly to the research training of graduate students in the Department of Sociology.

PHILIP M. HAUSER, *Director*
Population Research & Training Center
University of Chicago

ACKNOWLEDGMENTS

THIS BOOK has grown out of research carried out at the E. Kaplan School of Economics and Social Sciences, The Hebrew University of Jerusalem, a doctoral dissertation submitted to the Department of Sociology, The University of Chicago, and research conducted during a year spent as Research Associate, Population Research and Training Center, University of Chicago.

My initial opportunity to participate in demographic and social research in Israel was due mainly to Roberto Bachi, Professor of Statistics at the Hebrew University and Government Statistician of Israel, and his consistent interest, encouragement, and readiness to render assistance are gratefully acknowledged. Professor Don Patinkin, Dean of the E. Kaplan School, and Mr. Asher Reshef, former Executive Secretary of the Hebrew University, were instrumental in arranging for the visits to Chicago in 1961-62 and 1963-64 during which the doctoral dissertation and this book were completed. Professors Philip M. Hauser, Elihu Katz, and Harrison C. White served as the dissertation committee at the University of Chicago and were unreservedly generous with their time and help. Mr. Alexander J. Morin, President of Aldine Publishing Co., first suggested and patiently encouraged the reworking of the doctoral dissertation into its present form. Miss Hana Okamoto, Administrative Secretary of the Population Research and Training Center, oversaw all the technical details of preparation of the manuscript; and Miss Jane Sjoman undertook the task of checking and correcting the manuscript.

Much of the census and other research data that provides the basis for this book was also used in preparing a research

report for the Population Reference Bureau that is scheduled
to be published in a forthcoming issue of the *Population Bulletin*. Insofar as there is duplication among these materials, I
gratefully acknowledge the permission of the Population Reference Bureau to make use of them for the present present purpose.

My greatest indebtedness is to my two teachers and
friends: Shmuel Ettinger, Professor of Jewish History at the
Hebrew University, and Philip M. Hauser, Professor of Sociology and Director of the Population Research and Training
enter, University of Chicago. Neither study, nor research, nor
writing could have been undertaken without the opportunities,
encouragement, and intellectual guidance which they have
provided. Finally it is a pleasure to acknowledge the interest
and assistance of friends, colleagues, and students both in the
Kaplan School at the Hebrew University of Jerusalem and in
the Department of Sociology at the University of Chicago.

Jerusalem, Israel   J. M.
The Hebrew University
May, 1965

CONTENTS

INTRODUCTION:
THE SOCIAL STRUCTURE
OF JEWISH COMMUNITIES

THE MODERN EPIC of Israel recounts the remarkable growth of the Jewish population, the drama of the "ingathering of the exiles" and of efforts to absorb the hundreds of thousands of immigrants from scores of countries, linguistic backgrounds, and cultures; two wars, chronic tension and differences with the antagonistic neighboring Arab states, and the perpetual necessity of maintaining her military alertness and preparedness. All these have captured for Israel the interest and attention of journalists and their readers, of spiritual leaders and their flocks, of politicians and their supporters, and of fundraisers and their contributors. Not least of all, Israel's growth and her social, economic, and political problems have drawn the attention of social scientists: some have come to Israel to carry out research and many others have demonstrated active interest in and support of social scientific research in and concerning Israel.

But social scientists, perhaps taking the notion of "Israel as a social-scientific laboratory" somewhat too seriously somewhat too soon, have too frequently sought answers in Israel to the very most general and abstract problems and issues of sociology and the social sciences; and often they have neglected the task of *description* of social structure and patterns of social change in Israel. The purpose of this book is to try to specify some of the main characteristics and dimensions of social structure in Israel and to inquire in what manner, to what extent, and in what directions these have been changing in recent years. In so far as they are available, *data* bearing upon description and analysis of social change in Israel will be examined or referred to. An effort will be made to indicate or suggest directions for further empirical research in Israel—both in order to generate new and additional data and to exploit and learn from the data already available but largely unanalyzed.

Before proceeding some preliminary notes seem in order concerning description and characterizations of social structure in general, characterizations of social structures of Jewish communities in particular, and their relationships to specification, description, or analysis of social structure and social change in contemporary Israel. The rest of this first chapter is devoted to these preliminary conceptual and procedural notes. The second chapter reviews the growth and settlement of the Jewish population of Palestine and Israel from the last decades of the previous century until Israel's recent (May 1961) population census. Three following chapters deal with change in the religious and political spheres, in the educational and occupational spheres, and in family formation and organization. A summary chapter concludes the book.

The point of view of this book holds, very generally, that description, characterization, or specification of the social structure of a given society ought to include

1. identification and description of the content of the most important social roles;

2. analysis of the organization of the important social roles and of interrelationships in social systems and subsystems located at or oriented to the various levels of social organization; and

3. analysis of the composition of the population of the society by social roles or by combinations of roles, including analysis of the major axes of differentiation of the population by social roles or combinations of roles.[1]

1. The concept "role" is used here in the sense of S. F. Nadel, *The Theory of Social Structure* (Glencoe: The Free Press, 1957); "social system" is used in the sense of T. Parsons, *The Social System* (Glencoe:

Application of this scheme to description and analysis of any real or actual society or social collectivity is necessarily beset with difficulties and can, at best, achieve only partial descriptions, characterizations, or specifications of the social structure or the changes in social structure. In particular the application of this scheme to analysis of Jewish communities encounters two problems: 1. availability of data, and 2. interpretation of the particular relationship obtaining between the Jewish minority group and the non-Jewish majority collectivity in the community being studied. It seems reasonable to assume that the relationship with the non-Jewish community ordinarily may be expected to influence the nature and content of the roles institutionalized in the Jewish community, their organization in social systems and subsystems, and the composition of the Jewish population by roles or by social categories; but often the exact form or direction of these influences can only be surmised.

It would appear self-evident that any attempt to deal with social change in post-independence Israel must begin with some sort of initial or "benchmark" characterization of the social structure of the Jewish community of pre-independence Palestine. The attempt to reconstruct and outline the main characteristics of the social structure of the *Yishuv*, the Jewish community of pre-independence Palestine, encounters two major kinds of difficulties. In the first place, certain basic data concerning social and economic characteristics are absent, e.g., working force attachment, marital status, family size and composition, educational attainment, languages, etc. Some demographic and socio-economic statistical data are available,[2] but cross-classifications giving demographic and socio-

The Free Press, 1951); and "level of social organization" is used in the sense of T. Parsons, "General Theory in Sociology," in R. K. Merton, et al. (eds.), *Sociology Today* (New York: Basic Books, 1959).

2. The main sources of statistical data relating to the *Yishuv* in the last years of the British Mandate are: Government of Palestine, *A Survey of Palestine* (2 vols., Jerusalem: Government Printer, 1946); Jewish Agency for Palestine, *Statistical Handbook of Jewish Palestine, 1947* (Jerusalem: Government Printer, 1947); Government of Palestine, *Statistical Abstract of Palestine, 1944-45* (Jerusalem: Government Printer,

economic characteristics of major population categories (other than for Jews and for non-Jews) are very rarely given. In the second place, the overwhelming majority of descriptive and analytical accounts of the *Yishuv* tend to be biased by political and ideological interests, and aspects of the social structure less obviously related to political developments in Palestine or to mobilization of financial or ideological support are relatively neglected. Thus, for example, there is an enormous literature concerning the organization of *kibbutzim,* the famous collective settlements, but relatively little information concerning, say, organization of urban religious communities; and very much has been written regarding Jewish political action vis-à-vis the Mandatory Government, but almost nothing concerning family structure; and so forth.

Of particular interest here is the tendency in the sociological analyses of the *Yishuv* undertaken thus far to equate the social structure of the *Yishuv* with the social structure of the Zionist movement, organizations, political parties, and institutions in Palestine during the Mandatory period. This tendency has had quite important consequences for the analysis of the absorption of immigrants and of social change in Israel.[3] According to this line of analysis, the Zionist organizations and political parties initiated, organized, and controlled Jew-

---

1946); and Jewish Agency for Palestine, *The Jewish Case Before the Anglo-American Committee of Inquiry on Palestine* (Jerusalem: Jewish Agency, 1947).

3. The most important examples are: S. N. Eisenstadt, "The Process of Absorption of Immigrants in Israel," in C. Frankenstein (ed.), *Between Past and Future* (Jerusalem: Henrietta Szold Foundation, 1953); S. N. Eisenstadt, *The Absorption of Immigrants* (London: Routledge and Kegan Paul, 1954); S. N. Eisenstadt, "The Social Conditions of the Development of Voluntary Associates—A Case Study of Israel," in R. Bachi (ed.), *Scripta Hierosolymitana,* Vol. III (Jerusalem: The Magnes Press, The Hebrew University, 1956); J. Ben-David, "Professions and Social Structure in Israel," in *ibid.;* S. N. Eisenstadt and J. Ben-David, "Intergeneration Tensions in Israel," *International Social Science Bulletin,* VIII, No. 1 (1956); Alex Weingrod, "From the Millah to the Moshav" (unpublished Ph.D. dissertation, Department of Anthropology, University of Chicago, 1959); and Moshe Lissak, "Trends in Occupational Choice Among Urban Youth in Israel," (unpublished Ph.D. dissertation, Department of Sociology, The Hebrew University of Jerusalem, 1961).

ish immigration to Palestine; they obtained recognition from the League of Nations and from the Mandatory Power as spokesmen and representatives of Jewish interests in Palestine; they initiated, organized, and controlled the educational system, a federation of trade unions, agricultural colonization, and the key political, economic, and cultural institutions in the *Yishuv;* and they were the loci of positions of power, influence, and prestige, and hence provided the major avenues of mobility, in the *Yishuv.* Economic differentiation existed in the *Yishuv,* but it is held, according to this analysis, to have been relatively independent of social prestige, political power, and control of allocation of resources and facilities created in the *Yishuv* or available from foreign sources. Both economic differentiation and social and political differentiation are held to have been independent of country-of-origin and of duration-of-residence in Palestine. Successive waves of immigrants to the *Yishuv* are asserted to have been absorbed rapidly in the economic and social structure and in no sense segregated residentially, in the economy, or in the social or political structure. In particular, new immigrants to the *Yishuv* are held to have been fully absorbed into the various subsystems and activities of the Zionist organizations and political parties, whence it follows—according to this line of analysis—that they were fully absorbed in and distributed within the various spheres of the social structure of the *Yishuv.*

This analysis of the *Yishuv* will be considered again in the final chapter. For the moment it is important especially to note that what may be called the *Yishuv*-qua-Zionist-enterprise analysis falls short of meeting some of the desiderata indicated above for a satisfactory characterization of the social structure of the *Yishuv.* In the first place, only the social roles having or construed to have some connection with the Zionist economic and political enterprise (i.e., establishment of a viable economy based upon Jewish labor and enterprise and promotion and defense of Jewish political interests in Palestine vis-à-vis the Mandatory Government, the Arab communities, and the outside world) are seen as relevant. Other social roles, most notably family and kinship roles, are neglected. Secondly, social subsystems and arenas of social interaction other than those of the Zionist organizations, political parties, and various institutions are systematically neglected. Aside from families, neighborhood and voluntary associations, and other informal groupings, other such subsystems with probably fairly elaborate structures include the so-called private sector of the economy, the religious community, and possibly the Jewish employees of the Palestinian civil service. Part of the religious community was anti-Zionist, consistently boycotted the recognized community organs, and sought separate recognition from the Mandatory Government.

There is very little consideration of the composition of the *Yishuv* with respect to social roles and to extent of participation in the Zionist enterprises and activities. Such consideration as is given to this question seems ordinarily intended to document the assertion of high levels of such participation rather than to analyze structural components in the *Yishuv*. (If it was in fact true, as claimed by the General Labor Federation, the *Histadruth*, that seventy-five percent of Jewish wage and salary workers in Palestine were members of that organization, then it was likewise true that twenty-five percent *were not* members; but the latter group has received very little, if any, attention and interest.) Finally, there is an implicit and sometimes explicit assumption of general accessibility for all persons in the *Yishuv* to all types of roles in the Zionist enterprise. The differentiation supposedly occurs on the basis of participation in appropriate pioneering activities (i.e., *kibbutz* members are more likely to achieve key positions than non-*kibbutz* members, but anyone may be a *kibbutz* member if he wishes). Differentiation outside the Zionist enterprise is presumed of only minimal relevance to the social structure of the *Yishuv*. This assumption seems based upon Zionist ideologies and is not subjected to any systematic investigation.

As indicated above, the attempt to characterize the social structure of the *Yishuv* is beset by real difficulties in terms of availability of data.[4] But, perhaps more important, the *Yishuv*-qua-Zionist-enterprise analysis has systematically neglected those components of the social structure of the *Yishuv* not directly involved in the political emergence of the State of Israel. This is neither to detract from the achievements of the Zionist movement nor to question the legitimacy of a "sociology of Zionism," but to indicate an area requiring much more investigation than has taken place to date. As it happens, those components of the social structure of the *Yishuv* not involved in the political emergence of the State of Israel very often *are* involved in the process of absorption of new immigrants and very often *are* involved in social change taking place in Israel.

A second more or less obvious starting point in dealing with social change in Israel is the analysis of the social structure of the Jewish communities from which immigrants to Palestine and Israel originated. There is no group of Jews known anywhere in the world which is distributed "at random" among its non-Jewish neighbors and which is lacking in some distinctive social characteristics. Regardless of their political status in the host communities, Jews have always been characterized by one or another demographic or socio-economic pattern different in at least some respect from the pattern of the non-Jewish communities. In particular, the Jewish communities in Europe and in the Islamic countries of Africa and the Middle East (the main sources of the post-independence mass immigration to Israel) were for generations ethnic minorities with distinctive communal structures and institutionalized relationships with the non-Jewish majorities.

In the case of the European Jewish communities, historians have long studied the political, social, and economic relationships with the non-Jewish host societies, internal and

4. Certain data bearing upon the social structure of the *Yishuv* have become available *since* Israel's independence, especially in connection with activities of the Central Bureau of Statistics and the E. Kaplan School of Economics and Social Science of the Hebrew University, and some of these data will be considered in later chapters.

communal organization (including educational, religious and welfare institutions, the Zionist movement, marriage and the family), and composition by economic characteristics. Rich materials are available concerning these components of the social structures of the European Jewish communities prior to World War II.[5]

Much less is known about the social structure of the Jewish communities in Islamic countries. However, there has lately been great interest in these communities, and two general kinds of patterns emerge from recent researches.[6] The first pattern is that of a traditional society, relatively untouched by urbanism, secular education, or technology. It is characterized by strong emphasis upon kinship and extended family organization, low status of women, community leadership vested in religious personages, and relative isolation from the non-Jewish host communities. The second pattern is that of a society in transition, newly urbanized and partially secularized, with increasing emphasis upon nuclear families and a breakdown of extended family bonds. There are economic and some social and political relationships with the non-Jewish community on a much broader front, some competition with emerging Moslem middle-classes, bureaucrats, petty-traders, etc., and conflicts for power and leadership between the traditional religious figures and the emergent secularized elite. In both patterns, the Jewish communities are characterized by low economic, educational, and health levels, by recurring problems of physical security, and by ambiguities of orientation in

5. See, for example, the bibliographical materials in *Jewish Year Book* (London: Jewish Chronicle Publications, 1894-), published annually; also, A. Ruppin, *Soziologie der Jüden* (2 vols., Berlin: Jüdischer Verlag, 1930), trans. as *The Jews in the Modern World* (London: Macmillan, 1934).

6. See, for example, Jewish Agency, "The Position of the Jewish Communities in Oriental Countries," and "The Situation of Iraqi Jewry," in Jewish Agency, *The Jewish Case . . . op. cit.*; A. Weingrod, *op. cit.*; S. D. Gotein, "Jewish Education in Yemen," in C. Frankenstein (ed.), *Between Past and Future, op. cit.*; and R. Patai, *Israel Between East and West* (Philadelphia: Jewish Publication Society, 1953). The distinction between the two patterns follows that made by S. N. Eisenstadt, *The Absorption of Immigrants, op. cit.*, pp. 118-119.

conflicts between emergent indigenous nationalism and European conquerers or protectors. For the communities in the Islamic countries certain economic and political roles defined with reference to the Moslem host societies, certain family and communal roles, etc., may be identified in a general way. But the content of these roles, their organization in subsystems, the composition of the populations with respect to these social roles, and the types and bases of differentiation remain obscure and cannot at present be plotted even in their barest outlines.

Thus far it has seemed reasonable to presume that the origins of the social structure in contemporary Israel lie in the social structure of the *Yishuv*, the Jewish community in pre-independence Palestine, and in the social structures of the Jewish communities abroad from which the present Jewish population of Israel largely originates. But two important though quite distinct problems arise in any attempt to relate these to present social structure in Israel. The first is a problem of sorting or selectivity: i.e., the social structure of survival through wars and mass persecution, the social structure of migration and emigration, and the extent to which the various social roles and institutions of the Jewish communities abroad are retained or lost, transferred or left behind, preserved intact or transformed in the processes of survival and migration. The second is a problem of the nature of the changes in social structure of a collectivity that is transformed from a "marginal" to a "non-marginal" group. The marginal group is functionally specialized and segregated but integrated within and economically dependent upon some larger collectivity. The non-marginal collectivity is economically "independent" with all of the roles and systems of roles vital to its very physical survival occupied by members of that collectivity.

The problem of sorting and selectivity, of the social structure, of survival and migration derives especially from the tragic history of European Jewry during World War II. But it is also connected with more recent developments in the political and economic status of Jews in the Middle Eastern, North African, and Central Asiatic countries (i.e., "Oriental"

Jews), and of Jews in Central and Eastern Europe. Of the pre-war communities in every country on the European continent only the Bulgarian, Danish, Finnish, and Swedish Jewish communities survived World War II more or less intact. All the others were devastated by deportations and extermination. There is an obvious demographic-accounting problem involved in tracing the numbers in the various pre-war Jewish communities and their distribution by histories or fates during and after World War II: of all the pre-war communities in the different countries, and of the "natural increase" during the World War II period—the number of survivors and non-survivors to, say, 1948; of the survivors—the number remaining in or returning to countries of birth, the number immigrating to Palestine or Israel, and the number migrating elsewhere.

While data for carrying out such a demographic reconstruction of the survival and movement of the Jewish population of Europe are not so readily available for all countries or communities, nevertheless the problem is conceptually straightforward enough. The total number of Jews of a given geographic origin presently alive in their countries of birth, in Israel, in the United States, in the Soviet Union, etc., represents the total number of survivors of the pre-war Jewish community (and its "natural increase") in that geographic location; and the difference between this total and the total pre-war population (plus its expected "natural increase") represents the number of non-survivors.

Data on the size of populations of most pre-war European Jewish communities are available, and, at least hypothetically, it is possible to conceive of a count or an estimate of current survivors and of their distribution by current place of residence, so that such an analysis may in fact be carried out even if only in vague outline. Table 1.1 indicates some of the elements of the analysis which plots the relationship between pre-war European communities, survival, migration, and the composition of the present population of Israel.

A much more difficult problem, both conceptually and

TABLE 1.1.

HYPOTHETICAL TABLE SHOWING JEWISH POPULATION BY COUNTRY OF ORIGIN, SURVIVAL IN WORLD WAR II, AND COUNTRY OF RESIDENCE IN 1960

| | JEWISH POPULATION: 1939-1945 | | | | JEWISH POPULATION, 1960 | | | | | |
COUNTRY OF ORIGIN (PRE-WW II)	Jewish Population in 1939 (1)	Expected Natural Increase, 1939-1945 (2)	Jewish Population in 1945 (3)	Estimated Non-Survivors (3) − [(1) + (2)] (4)	Total All Countries (5)	In Israel (6)	In USA (7)	In USSR (8)	In Country of Origin (9)	In Other Countries (10)
Total—All Countries										
Country A										
Country B										
Country C										
.										
.										
.										

11

practically, is the relationship between the social structure
of the pre-war European communities and that of contemporary Israel. As mentioned above, information is available in
considerable detail concerning the social structure of at least
some of the pre-war European Jewish communities. For many
Jewish communities it is possible to plot or characterize their
social structure. We can list and describe major social roles,
social subsystems and institutions, and composition of the
population by roles and by major spheres of activity. However,
the relationship between social structure of the pre-war Jewish
communities and that of Israel is mediated by: 1. differential rates of survival, 2. differential rates of migration to Israel,
and 3. differential rates of preservation of role and institutional
content which are associated with the respective roles and
institutions.

Assuming, for the purpose of simplicity, that some single
set of exhaustive and mutually exclusive social categories can
serve for all the pre-war and post-war Jewish communities,
then the relationship between the composition of the population of contemporary Israel by social categories and that of
pre-war European communities might be derived in the form
of Table 1.2. But oversimplified as it is, Table 1.2 is, of course,
much more complicated than the previous table; for what is
required is information on differential rates of survival or non-
survival in the war, differential rates of migration to the
various possible countries of immigration, and differential
rates of remaining within the initial social category or of
moving to each of the alternative social categories.

More difficult than the sheer complexity of the information
required for such an analysis is the fact that the differential
rates of survival, migration, change of category, etc., cannot
ordinarily be inferred from comparison of pre-war populations
with post-war survivors in the various countries, since net
changes could be effected by any of these phenomena separately or in combination. But, rather, only data and information bearing directly upon survival and migration of persons
in the various social categories or having the various roles

TABLE 1.2.

HYPOTHETICAL TABLE SHOWING JEWISH POPULATION BY COUNTRY AND SOCIAL CATEGORY OF ORIGIN, SURVIVAL IN WORLD WAR II, AND BY COUNTRY OF RESIDENCE AND SOCIAL CATEGORY IN 1960

COUNTRY AND SOCIAL CATEGORY OF ORIGIN (PRE-WW II)	JEWISH POPULATION: 1939-1945			
	Jewish Population in 1939 (1)	*Expected Natural Increase, 1939-1945* (2)	*Jewish Population in 1945* (3)	*Estimated Non-Survivors* $(3) - [(1) + (2)]$ (4)
Total—All Countries				
Total				
Soc. Category 1				
" 2				
" 3				
.				
.				
.				
Country A				
Total				
Soc. Category 1				
" 2				
" 3				
.				
.				
.				
Country B				
Total				
Soc. Category 1				
" 2				
" 3				
.				
.				
.				

TABLE 1.2. Cont.

JEWISH POPULATION BY COUNTRY OF RESIDENCE AND SOCIAL CATEGORY, 1960

COUNTRY AND SOCIAL CATEGORY OF ORIGIN (PRE-WW II)	Total—All Countries			In Israel			In USA			In USSR			In Country of Origin			In Other Countries		
	Total All Soc. Cat.	Soc. Cat. 1	Soc. Cat. 2 ...	Total All Soc. Cat.	Soc. Cat. 1	Soc. Cat. 2 ...	Total All Soc. Cat.	Soc. Cat. 1	Soc. Cat. 2 ...	Total All Soc. Cat.	Soc. Cat. 1	Soc. Cat. 2 ...	Total All Soc. Cat.	Soc. Cat. 1	Soc. Cat. 2 ...	Total All Soc. Cat. ...	Soc. Cat. 1	Soc. Cat. 2 ...
	(3a)	(5b)	(5c) ...	(6a)	(6b)	(6c) ...	(7a)	(7b)	(7c) ...	(8a)	(8b)	(8c) ...	(9a)	(9b)	(9c) ...	(10a) ...	(10b)	(10c) ...

Total—All Countries

Total

  Soc. Cat. 1
    "   " 2
    "   " 3
    .   .   .

Country A
  Total

  Soc. Cat. 1
    "   " 2
    "   " 3
    .   .   .

Country B
  Total

  Soc. Cat. 1
    "   " 2
    "   " 3
    .   .   .

and upon preservation of, or change in, the content of the various roles will permit filling in the analyses represented in Table 1.2. It is, of course, always possible to infer or to guess that, say, certain political party roles in contemporary Israel are carry-overs from European Jewish community political activity, especially Zionist party activity, in pre-World War I years, while other roles, say, certain agricultural or other manual occupational roles, are, for Jews, indigenous to-Palestine or Israel. Direct investigations of the social structure of survival and migration of European Jewry, and of the transfer of social roles or institutions to Israel, should and can be carried out; and such investigation would help clarify both the origins and the nature of the social structure of the Jewish community in Palestine and Israel.

In a similar vein analysis of the social structure of migration of Oriental Jewry to Israel, and of differential preservation, transfer, or transformation of characteristic social roles, subsystems, and institutions would contribute to understanding of the structure of these immigrant groups in Israel and of the relative importance of their various roles and institutions. Indeed, some beginnings in this direction have been undertaken recently, and some of the data available and analyses presented will be reviewed in later chapters.

To recapitulate: the relationship between the social structures, known or unknown, of Jewish communities abroad and that of the Jewish population of Palestine and Israel is mediated by differential rates of survival through World War II and by differential rates of migration to Israel characteristic of the various social subgroups of the Jewish communities abroad—i.e., by what has been called the "social structure of survival and migration." Analysis of the social structure of survival and migration presents both conceptual and data-collection problems; but a more systematic attack on this problem is likely to yield both important information regarding the processes involved and important insights into the origins and formation of the social structure of Israel.

There is a second type of problem in relating the social

structure of the *Yishuv* (the Jewish community in pre-independence Palestine) and of Jewish communities abroad to
that of Israel at present or at some earlier date. It involves
assessing of the effect of the transformation of the Jewish
populations and immigrant groups comprising Israeli society
from a "marginal," dependent, functionally specialized social
collectivity essentially segregated in some subsection of a larger
viable social structure into increasingly a "non-marginal,"
independent, functionally diffuse society with members of the
collectivity filling the entire array of roles and functions of a
viable society. In general it is held here that any population
or society must organize—in the sense of social organization
and of economic organization—to adapt collectively to survive
in its geographic, physical, or material environment. In the
absence of institutional or physical-material barriers or inhibit-
ing factors (factors raising mortality or lowering fertility),
populations tend to grow and increase. Every collectivity
must institutionalize some social and economic roles and
subsystems, both to assure physical survival and to protect or
promote "vital interests" in the face of actual or potential
pressure of numbers upon the resources immediately at hand.
The above does not specify what *are* the "vital interests" other
than survival, who specifies them for the collectivity or society,
or what is their importance or weight relative to survival
requirements. The description and analysis of the variation
in these areas is surely one of the tasks of sociology. For
example, a society may view as a "vital interest" such varied
values as national power or prestige, individual freedom,
leisure, knowledge, wealth, art, etc. The relative importance
to a society of these values, and the society's action taken to
promote them, may be determined by collective institutions
of the entire society (say voting or referenda), by some individual ruler, or by a ruling class, oligarchy, etc.

Historically Jewish communities have been attached to,
and have had physical sustenance and survival assured by,
the adaptive, technological-economic arrangements of the
larger host societies. For Jewish communities physical and

communal survival was typically dependent not upon effective filling of, say, "technological" roles, but rather upon filling effectively the "political" and "economic" roles mediating the relationship between Jews and non-Jews on the one hand, and the internal "educational" roles promoting cohesiveness and separatism of the community. To a considerable extent, the Zionist back-to-the-soil ideologies not withstanding, a balance between "survival" and other "vital interest" roles not so very dissimilar to those of Jewish communities abroad obtained in the *Yishuv* prior to independence. Evidently the economy of the Jewish community in Palestine was to a very large extent tied to the policies and initiative of the Mandatory regime and British colonial economic policy, to initiative, investment, and support of Jewish organizations and individuals abroad, and to the economy of the rural Arab population.

The Jewish community in contemporary Israel is, in this respect, a more "normal" community than were Jewish communities abroad or than was the *Yishuv*. This is the case at least to the extent that physical and material survival are dependent in much greater measure upon local decision, initiative, and implementation, i.e., upon *members* of the society or collectivity filling the entire range of social or economic roles assuring the society's physical or material "survival" or adaptation.

Israel is evidently witness to rising prestige associated with "production" or "technological" roles, or with roles related to economic organization, defense, etc. There is a corresponding decline of "rabbi-teacher-moral-leader" roles, and of the "ethnic group" roles associated with mediation of ethnic group relationships with the total society and with promoting separatism and internal cohesion. For the ethnic groups segregated in a larger collectivity sustenance and material survival or welfare were either taken largely for granted or were not in the province of direction or initiative of the ethnic collectivity *qua* ethnic collectivity (though individuals, of course, could be prominent in economic roles). "Vital interests" other than

sustenance, technological or physical-material adaptation normally capture the attention and prestige in the ethnic group,
although the ethnic "captain of industry," famous politician,
great soldier, or incumbent of a role normally not accessible
to the ethnic group does enjoy great personal prestige in the
group. But "soldier" or "national politician" or "captain of
industry" are not normally roles directly crucial to the survival, or, indeed, to the "vital interest" of the ethnic group
qua ethnic group.

Thus specification of a "benchmark" social structure of
the Jewish population of Israel in its earliest years, which
would normally take account of the social structure of the
Jewish community of pre-independence Palestine, the *Yishuv*,
and of the social structure of the Jewish communities from
which post-independence immigrants originated is rendered
particularly problematic in three respects. In the first place,
adequate descriptions of the social structure of the *Yishuv*
and of the Oriental Jewish communities abroad are absent.
In the second place, the relationship between the social
structures of Jewish communities abroad and that of early
post-independence Israel is mediated by the social structure
or selectivity of survival through World War II and of
migration to Israel or elsewhere, processes whose barest outlines are virtually uncharted. Finally, the very transition from
marginality, in an ecological sense, to independence of the
Jewish community in Israel necessarily effected certain trans-
formations in social and economic structure, the exact or even
approximate patterns of which are, for the time being, not
possible to trace, much less to separate from the effects of
growth and immigration.

Accordingly, the procedure in the succeeding chapters
will be as follows: Chapter 2 comprises a review of the growth
of the Jewish population of Israel and the growth of the
various types of settlement in Israel. In that chapter the bases
of age, geo-cultural origin, duration of residence, and type-
of-settlement differentiation are sketched. The chapter is
primarily an attempt to synthetize demographic and other

data from various sources by way of presenting a preliminary ecological outline of the structure of the Jewish population of Israel circa 1961 and indicating the trends leading to that structure. Chapter 3 considers the problem of social bases of political party organization and electoral support and recent changes therein. Chapter 4 describes occupational roles, the composition of the various sectors of the population by work attachments and occupational roles, and processes of change in occupational structure. The latter processes include recruitment to the various occupational categories and its relationship to intergenerational occupational mobility and to educational opportunities. Chapter 5 deals with changing patterns of marriage, family formation, and family structure. Particular attention is given to data showing correlates of what has been termed "rationalization of family formation," and these in turn are related to elements of demographic and socio-economic structure outlined in earlier chapters. Chapter 6 tries to recapitulate the main points of the earlier chapters, summarize the descriptive notes on the social structure of Israel, and review the main directions of change. The points made in this first chapter are reviewed in the light of the more detailed data and materials of the intervening chapters and restated in the form of an overview of social change in Israel.

2

THE JEWISH POPULATION:
GROWTH, EXPANSION OF SETTLEMENT,
AND CHANGING COMPOSITION

I. INTRODUCTION

ISRAEL'S FIRST full-fledged Census of Population was carried out on May 22, 1961, and, according to the official census results, the Jewish population of Israel on that date totaled 1,932,357. The earliest modern country-wide census in what is now Israel was carried out in 1922 by the British Mandatory Government of Palestine, and that census recorded a total of 83,794 Jewish residents. Between the earliest census in 1922 and the latest census in 1961 two other population counts were undertaken: in 1931 the British Mandatory Government carried out a second census of the population of Palestine which recorded a total of 174,610 Jewish residents; and in 1948 the Provisional Government of Israel carried out a "Registration of the Population" for the purpose of preparing lists of eligible voters in the elections to Israel's first parliament (*Knesset*). A total of 716,678 Jewish inhabitants were recorded in that registration.

In Table 2.1 it is seen that the Jewish population of Israel grew about twenty-four-fold in the thirty-nine-year interval between the first and latest censuses, although the growth rates were by no means uniform in all periods.

The next two sections of this chapter review the growth of the Jewish population of Palestine and Israel, emphasizing especially the most important component of that growth, immigration of Jews from scores of countries on every continent to Palestine and Israel. The fourth section describes the growth and changes in patterns of Jewish settlement and residence in Israel since attainment of independence in 1948; the fifth section compares socio-economic characteristics of veteran settlers and new immigrants, and of the major geo-cultural origin groups.

II. GROWTH OF THE JEWISH POPULATION OF PALESTINE TO 1948

Very little detailed information is available regarding the exact size, composition, or characteristics of the population of Palestine prior to the current century. The Turks, who ruled Palestine until the close of World War I, never carried out a census of any sort in the country. Such data as are available to demographers and historians derive from the descrip-

TABLE 2.1.

CENSUS COUNTS OF JEWISH POPULATION OF PALESTINE AND ISRAEL, 1922-1961

| | | TOTAL JEWISH POPULATION | INCREASE SINCE PREVIOUS CENSUS OR REGISTRATION | | |
| | | | | *Percent* | |
			Number	*Total*	*Average Annual*
Palestine:	Census, 1922	83,794	—		
Palestine:	Census, 1931	174,610	90,816	108.4	12.04
Israel Population Registration, 1948		716,678	542,068	310.4	18.26
Israel:	Census, 1961	1,932,357	1,215,679	169.6	13.05

Source: 1922 and 1931—Government of Palestine, *A Survey of Palestine* (2 Vols., Jerusalem: Government Printer, 1946), Vol. I. Table 7c, p. 149; 1948 and 1961—State of Israel, Central Bureau of Statistics, *Demographic Characteristics of the Population.* Part I (Population and Housing Census 1961, Publication No. 7, Jerusalem, 1962) Table 1, p. 3.

tive accounts of travelers, diplomats, missionaries, etc., and from research of contemporary historians.

A Jewish community has continuously existed in Palestine at least since the Middle Ages, and some historians believe that Jews have lived continuously in Palestine since ancient times. The total population of Palestine in the year 1800 is believed to have included some 300,000 persons, of which an estimated 5,000 were Jews, 25,000 were Christians, and the rest, an estimated 270,000 persons, were Moslems. The Jewish population was mostly of *Sephardic* (Spanish) origin and lived in the four "holy cities," Jerusalem, Safad, Tiberias, and Hebron. The Christian population was mostly Greek Orthodox, Greek Catholic, and Roman Catholic and resided principally in the cities of Jerusalem, Nazareth, and Bethlehem.

The Jewish population in Palestine, evidently benefiting from improvements in political, social, economic, and sanitary conditions, grew steadily during the nineteenth century, reaching an estimated 11,800 persons in 1845 and 24,000 persons in 1882. By that year a sizable Jewish community had arisen in the port city of Jaffa in addition to those in the cities already noted. The Jewish population of Palestine during this period was, by and large, extremely orthodox, and the communities were organized primarily around religious groupings (*kollelim*), each with institutions such as synagogues, schools, *yeshivot* (rabbinical seminaries), and religious charitable organizations.

A number of accounts of the earliest beginnings of the Zionist movement in Russia are available,[1] and it suffices here to note only that the beginnings of the modern Jewish immigration to Palestine followed a series of pogroms in Czarist Russia in 1880 and 1881 and coincided with the beginnings of a mass exodus of Jews from Russia. Hundreds of thousands of Russian Jews migrated westward, mostly to the United

1. See, for example, B. Halpern, *The Idea of a Jewish State* (Cambridge: Harvard University Press, 1961) and bibliography therein; also, B. Z. Dinaburg and S. Yavnieli (eds.), *Sefer Hatzionut* (Tel Aviv: Dvir, 1938); and N. Sokolow, *History of Zionism, 1600-1918* (London: Longman, Green and Co., 1919).

States but also to Central and Western European and Latin American countries, between 1880 and the beginning of World War I; and in 1882 a group of young persons, who named their group *Bilu* and were supported by the *Chovevei Zion* (Lovers of Zion) movement, immigrated to Palestine and later founded a Jewish agricultural settlement there. Despite difficulties and disappointments the group remained on the land and, indeed, was followed by additional settlers. The wave of immigrants and settlers which followed the initial immigration of the *Bilu* group in 1882 and continued until 1903 was called the "First *Aliyah*" (pl. *aliyot*), and in this First *Aliyah* between 20,000 and 30,000 Jewish immigrants arrived in Palestine.

By the close of the nineteenth century the interest of European Jewry in the revival of a Jewish national center in Palestine had become both much more intense and more widespread, and the World Zionist Organization had been founded. Beginning in 1904, Jewish immigration to Palestine took on new characteristics and dimensions. The new wave of immigrants consisted of organized groups of Russian and Polish Jews, many with socialist ideals and aspirations who were committed ideologically both to the re-establishment of a Jewish national existence in Palestine and to the creation of a society based upon the precepts of the European socialist tradition. In many instances these immigrants had been previously associated with the Eastern European socialist movements and had looked to the achievement of socialism in their respective countries of birth as a solution to the "Jewish problem," as well as to political, economic, and social problems in these countries generally.

The outbreak of a new wave of anti-Jewish pogroms in Russia and the failure of the socialist revolution in 1905 added impetus to the organization of socialist Zionist movements in Eastern Europe and to the wave of immigration to Palestine which continued from 1904 until the outbreak of World War I in 1914. This wave of immigration from 1904 through 1914 is usually denoted the "Second *Aliyah*," and with it came some 35,000 to 40,000 Jewish immigrants. The immigrants of the Second *Aliyah* brought with them to Palestine not only their powerful ties to Jewish history and traditions as well as to contemporary political and social movements and thought in their countries of origin, but also ideologies and principles concerning the nature and institutions of the Jewish community and society they intended to create. This wave of immigrants did in fact later become the political, social, economic, and ideological backbone of the Jewish community in Palestine, and large sectors of life in Israel today are organized around institutions created by immigrants arriving in the Second *Aliyah*.

The advent of World War I brought Jewish immigration to Palestine to a virtual halt. Indeed, the Turkish regime, which had brought the Ottoman Empire into the conflict on the side of the Axis powers, expelled numerous Zionists and citizens of Allied countries from Palestine. Others left the country because of extreme deterioration of health and economic conditions. The Jewish population of Palestine, which at the eve of World War I had reached 85,000 in number, was greatly reduced to some 56,000 persons by the time the war had ended.

During World War I the British armies occupied and took military control of Palestine and, with the dismembering of the Ottoman Empire at the close of the war, retained control over the territory. Throughout the war the World Zionist Organization had been increasingly active in promoting the national and political aspirations of the Zionist movement, and on November 2, 1917, the British Government formally expressed its sympathy with these aspirations through the issue of the Balfour Declaration. The latter was formally endorsed by the United States and embodied in the League of Nations' Mandate for Palestine in 1922 under which Britain officially undertook to place "the country under such political, administrative, and economic conditions as will secure the establishment of the Jewish National Home" in Palestine. The World Zionist Organization was recognized as the "appro-

priate Jewish agency for the purpose of advising and cooper-
ating with the Administration of Palestine in such economic,
social, and other matters as may affect the establishment of
the Jewish National Home."

The "Third *Aliyah*," the wave of immigrants arriving in the
years 1919 to 1923, was in certain respects the delayed com-
pletion of the Second *Aliyah*. This was also a wave of idealistic
pioneer immigrants, primarily from Russia, who had been
organized and prepared occupationally and ideologically even
before emigration from Europe. Although Jewish immigration
to Palestine was not completely unlimited by the Mandatory
Government (the criterion being the prospective immigrant's
likelihood to be absorbed into the economy), the political
developments mentioned above created a climate favorable
to Jewish immigration in the early years of the Mandate. In
addition the Bolshevik revolution in Russia brought additional
migratory pressure upon Jews in general and upon Zionists in
particular. In all, 35,000 Jews immigrated (the Mandatory
Government now maintaining statistics of immigration and
emigration—Table 2.2) to Palestine during the Third *Aliyah*,
an average of 7,000 annually.

Beginning in 1924 and continuing until 1931, some 82,000
immigrants, mostly middle-class Jews from Poland, arrived
in Palestine in the "Fourth *Aliyah*." An economic depression,
combined evidently with anti-Semitism, touched off widespread economic, social, and political sanctions and discrimination against the Jews in Poland and subjected them to
increasing pressure towards emigration. In the United States,
which had previously been the primary destination of Eastern
European overseas migrants, new legislation virtually excluded
additional immigrants from these countries, and large numbers of Polish Jews turned to Palestine.

During the Fourth *Aliyah* important numbers of Jews immigrated from non-European countries. Some 2,000 immigrants came from American countries, mostly from the United
States, and 9,200 immigrants arrived from Middle Eastern
countries, mostly from Iraq, Yemen and Aden, Persia, and

Turkey. In the Third *Aliyah* immigrants from non-Western countries (i.e., from Asian and African countries) had constituted just under five percent of all immigrants, but in the Fourth *Aliyah* the percentage of non-Western immigrants rose to twelve percent. In this period immigration to Palestine became a significant proportion of total worldwide Jewish migrations. Of a world total of some 393,000 Jewish migrants in the period, twenty-one percent immigrated to Palestine, compared to less than ten percent of all Jewish migrants during the period of the Third *Aliyah*. In Palestine itself an economic depression in the years 1926-1927 slowed down immigration and motivated a considerable number of Jews to emigrate to other countries. Thus during the Fourth *Aliyah*, although 82,000 immigrants arrived in the country, a total of 23,000 Jews emigrated from Palestine, and at the end of 1931 the Jewish population of Palestine numbered an estimated 175,000.

The years 1932-1938 witnessed the rise of the Nazis to power in Germany, the rapid movement of the great powers toward another global war, and an economic depression throughout the Western world. For the Jews of Central Europe, the period brought the beginnings of systematic political, social, and economic pressure which was later to become even more systematic extermination. At the same time economic hardship contributed to the increase of discriminatory pressures upon Jews in the Middle Eastern countries, especially in Yemen and Aden.

From 1932 until 1938, the period of the "Fifth *Aliyah*," more than 217,000 Jewish immigrants came to Palestine. The largest numbers came from Poland (91,000) and from Germany and Austria (40,000), but large numbers of Jewish immigrants came from the Soviet Union (16,000), from Rumania (11,000), and from Yemen and Aden (7,000) as well. In this seven-year period Jewish immigration to Palestine assumed some characteristics of a mass migration: an average of 31,000 immigrants arrived annually; an annual average of ninety-nine immigrants per thousand Jewish residents of

TABLE 2.2.
JEWISH POPULATION OF PALESTINE: COMPONENTS OF GROWTH, 1919-1948

| PERIOD | POPULATION AT BEGIN-NING OF PERIOD | NUMBER | | | PERCENT DISTRIBUTION | | |
		Total Increase in Period	Natural Increase	Net Migra-tion	Total In-crease	Natural In-crease	Net Migra-tion
Total: 1919-1948	56,000	593,633	167,088	426,545	100.0	28.2	71.8
Third *Aliyah*: 1919-23	56,000	36,000	6,500	29,500	100.0	18.1	81.9
Fourth *Aliyah*: 1924-31	92,000	83,138	26,013	57,125	100.0	31.3	68.7
Fifth *Aliyah*: 1932-38	175,138	237,584	42,413	195,175	100.0	17.9	82.1
W.W. II: 1939-45	412,722	151,107	61,667	89,440	100.0	40.8	59.2
Post W.W. II: 1946-48	563,829	85,804	30,495	55,309	100.0	35.5	64.5
Israel Independence: 14.V.1948	649,633						

Source: M. Sicron, *Immigration to Israel, 1948-53*, Vol. II, Statistical Supplement, Tables A2, A3, Jerusalem, 1957.

Palestine arrived in this period (in the years 1933-1935, an annual average of 167 immigrants per thousand residents arrived); and of the worldwide Jewish migratory movements involving 380,000 persons in the period, immigration to Palestine constituted fifty-three percent, more than half the total.

Sources of immigrants, which in previous waves of immigration had been limited primarily to Jewish communities in Russia, Poland, and, to a small extent, to countries in the Middle East, now included many more Jewish communities. German and Austrian Jews, of whom very few had previously migrated to Palestine, came in large numbers in the face of a rapidly deteriorating political situation in those countries; the immigration from Rumania was more than double all previous immigration of Rumanian Jews; for the first time important numbers of Jews immigrated from Greece, Czechoslovakia, and Hungary, and immigration from North and South America was almost double that of the previous period.

The Fifth *Aliyah* was different from previous waves of immigration in other important respects. Immigrants in this period were older, there were relatively fewer single adults and relatively more family units, and the sex ratio was more "normal" than had been the case in previous waves. The Fifth *Aliyah* brought a large proportion of persons of means, businessmen, and members of the liberal professions. Of immigrants arriving in the period who had been gainfully employed abroad, a full thirty percent had been engaged either in commerce or in the liberal professions, compared to fourteen percent in the Fourth *Aliyah* and seventeen percent in the Third *Aliyah*. Immigrants of the Fifth *Aliyah*, with their capital and commercial initiative, founded a great many new enterprises in the country, and many important industries, commercial establishments, financial organizations, and cultural institutions in Israel today were begun by immigrants of the Fifth *Aliyah*.

As had been the case in previous periods of immigration, a certain number found life in Palestine difficult, adjustment to social and economic conditions very hard, and physical danger due to a period of Arab unrest. Some 19,000 persons emigrated from Palestine during this same period. At the close of the Fifth *Aliyah*, at the end of the year 1938, the Jewish population of Palestine totaled about 413,000.

By the last two years of the Fifth *Aliyah*, Jewish immigration to Palestine had slowed down, partly due to a series of Arab riots occurring in the years 1936-1939. These riots were directed against the Jewish population and against the British Mandatory Government, and in particular against the immigration policy which was permitting such a rapid increase in the proportion of Jews in the population of Palestine. In May, 1939, with the publication of the *White Paper on Palestine*, the British government restricted the number of Jewish immigrants to 15,000 annually for the following five years and declared further that after the five-year period "no further Jewish immigration will be permitted unless the Arabs of Palestine are prepared to acquiesce in it."

This policy continued throughout World War II, and in the years 1939-1945 only 46,000 European Jews were permitted legal entry into Palestine while another 29,000 entered "illegally." Polish, German, Rumanian, and Czech Jews constituted the bulk of the European immigrants, but a certain number also came from the Soviet Union, Bulgaria, Hungary, Austria, Yugoslavia, and Italy. In addition some 17,000 immigrants from non-European countries arrived in Palestine during World War II, so that the total Jewish immigration to Palestine during the seven-year period was 92,000, and the Jewish population totaled 564,000 at the end of the war.

The close of World War II found some 200,000 European Jews, mostly of Russian, Polish, and German origin, homeless and with virtually no prospect for resettlement in their countries of birth. These Jews, along with numbers of non-Jews in similar straits, were designated "Displaced Persons" by the Allied Powers, and temporary camps were established to provide them with food, shelter, and medical care. The British government stood fast in its refusal to permit further Jewish immigration to Palestine, and the immigration issue became a focal point of much political pressure, intrigue, negotiation, and action involving the Jews of Palestine, the British Government, the American Government, the United Nations, world Jewish organizations, and the newly established Arab governments. Throughout a period of investigations and inquiries, negotiations and conferences, a small stream of "illegal" immigration was organized and maintained by the Jews of Palestine. Of a total of 61,000 Jewish immigrants entering Palestine during the years 1946-1948, about 32,000 were permitted legally and 29,000 entered "illegally." Immigrants of this period came mostly from Poland, Rumania, Hungary, and Czechoslovakia and included relatively large proportions of single and unattached persons, and a very large proportion (62%) of young adults between the ages of fifteen and twenty-nine.

During the entire Mandatory Period (1919–May, 1948) a total of 487,000 Jewish immigrants arrived in Palestine, including about 53,000 persons who entered the country initially as travellers or tourists and remained as residents. Slightly under a third of all Jewish overseas migrants in this period immigrated to Palestine and, of these, eighty-seven percent came from Europe, ten percent from Asia (mostly from Middle Eastern countries), and three percent immigrated from North and South America, Africa, and Oceania. In the same period 60,000 Jews emigrated from Palestine to other countries, about fourteen percent of the total number of immigrants.

Since the Turkish authorities maintained no population statistics whatsoever for the period prior to the British Mandate over Palestine, it is impossible to determine the rate of natural increase of the Jewish population. However, for the Mandatory Period vital statistics are available; and in this period, from 1919 to 1948, the Jewish population of Palestine increased by 167,000 due to natural increase. In the period of the Third *Aliyah* (1919-1923) the population growth due to natural increase totaled 6,500, an annual average of 17.5 per thousand persons in the population. In the period following, that of the Fourth *Aliyah* (1924-1931), the excess of births over deaths increased the population by 26,000 or an annual average of 23.8 per thousand persons in the population. The average annual rate of natural increase in the period of the Fifth *Aliyah* (1932-1938) decreased to 20.5 per thousand, and the population growth due to natural increase was 42,000 in this period. During World War II the average annual rate of natural increase dropped further to 18.0 per thousand, but the total increase in population due to excess births over deaths was 62,000. In the final years of the British Mandate (1946-1948) the rate dropped even further to an average of 16.0 per thousand, and natural increase accounted for the addition of some 30,000 persons to the Jewish population during this period (Table 2.2).

Thus in the period from 1882, the beginning of organized immigration, until 1914, the outbreak of World War I, the Jewish population of Palestine more than tripled, growing from an estimated 24,000 in 1882 to 85,000 in 1914 and declining to 56,000 in 1919. Although between 55,000 and 70,-000 Jews immigrated to the country in this period, it is not known how many died or how many left the country. Similarly it is not known what portion of the net increase in population was due to immigration and what portion to natural increase. During the Mandatory Period, 1919-1948, the Jewish population of Palestine increased more than eleven-fold, growing from 56,000 in 1919 to 649,000 in May, 1948. Of the total increase of 593,000 during this period, seventy-two percent was due to net migration (the excess of immigrants over emigrants), and twenty-eight percent was accounted for by natural increase (the excess of births over deaths).

In November 1948, six months after the end of the Mandate and Israel's emergence as an independent state, the first enumeration of the population was conducted. The Jewish population of Israel in November, 1948, totaled 716,678 persons. Of these, thirty-five percent were Israel- (or Palestine-) born and sixty-five percent were born abroad. Of those born abroad, eighty-five percent were born in Europe, America, or Oceania, twelve percent were born in Asia (mostly the Middle East, excluding Palestine), and three percent were born in Africa (mostly North and Northeastern Africa). The population was, on the average, younger than populations of Western countries, but older than the populations of most Asian and African countries. More than half the population was concentrated in the three largest cities, Tel Aviv, Haifa, and Jerusalem, and about fifteen percent of the population lived in rural settlements.

III. JEWISH IMMIGRATION TO ISRAEL: 1948-1960[2]

It is appropriate to recall here that the central issue in the post-World War II conflict between the Jews of Palestine and the British Government (the Mandatory power), was precisely the continuation of Jewish immigration to Palestine. The Jews of Palestine, with rare exceptions, did not take issue with the Mandatory Power over civil rights, social equality, political self-determination, economic exploitation, lack of development, or depressed levels of living as may have been the case with other countries striving for independence. The issue was clearly Jewish immigration and fulfillment of the commitments of the Balfour Declaration and the League of Nations' Mandate. Thus it was the question of Jewish immigration to Palestine which generated the chain of events leading Great Britain to bring the question of the status of Palestine before the United Nations, the decision of the United Nations to sponsor the partition of Palestine into independent Jewish and Arab states, Great Britain's admin-

2. This review draws upon the excellent analysis by Sicron for the years 1948-1955 and upon publications of the Israel Central Bureau of Statistics for later years. See M. Sicron, *Immigration to Israel: 1948-1953* (2 vols., Jerusalem: Israel Central Bureau of Statistics, Special Series No. 60, 1957) and Israel Central Bureau of Statistics, *Statistical Abstract of Israel, Nos. 8-13* (Jerusalem: Israel Central Bureau of Statistics, 1956-1962). Israel Central Bureau of Statistics publications are cited hereafter as "CBS, *Stat. Abstract No. 8*," etc.

istrative and military withdrawal from Palestine, and the establishment on May 14, 1948, of an independent Jewish state, Israel.

In its very declaration of independence Israel repealed all limitations upon Jewish immigration and later formalized, in the 1950 *Law of Return*, the principle of the right of all Jews to immigrate to the country. While in the first months of independence, the months of the war against the invading Arab armies, immigration was limited to young pioneers and volunteers, by September, 1948, a mass immigration was under way. This mass immigration continued through 1951, bringing an average of 15,000 Jewish immigrants *monthly* to the new State of Israel, and totaling 687,000 immigrants in the four-year period, more than the entire pre-independence Jewish population (Table 2.3).

The first priority on the immigration agenda concerned the Jews in the Displaced Persons camps in Germany, Austria, and Italy, and in the period from September, 1948, to July, 1949, some fifty-two Displaced Persons camps were emptied in Germany alone. After actual residents of the camps emigrated, some of these camps remained transit centers for Jews not previously resident in camps but joining the stream of immigrants to Israel. In the winter of 1948/49 the last of the "illegal" immigrants who had been caught by British authorities and held in detention camps in Cyprus were brought to Israel. In that same winter practically the entire Bulgarian Jewish community and large proportions of the Turkish and Yugoslavian Jewish communities immigrated to Israel. At the same time news of the establishment of Israel spread to Jewish communities of French North Africa, and the stream of immigration from those countries was organized and begun.

The following year Poland and Rumania, which for a time had prohibited the emigration of Jews, again allowed them to emigrate. Although both these countries later again prohibited emigration, some 100,000 Polish Jews and 120,000 Rumanian Jews managed to immigrate to Israel during this

TABLE 2.3.

JEWISH POPULATION OF ISRAEL: COMPONENTS OF GROWTH, 1948-1961

YEAR	POPULATION AT BEGINNING OF PERIOD	NUMBER			PERCENT DISTRIBUTION		
		Total Increase	Natural Increase	Net Migration	Total Increase	Natural Increase	Net Migration
Total:							
15.V.48—31.XII.60	649,633	1,261,556	392,311	869,245	100.0	31.1	68.9
15.V.48—31.XII.48	649,633	109,068	4,588	104,480	100.0	4.2	95.8
1949	758,701	255,170	20,248	234,922	100.0	7.9	92.1
1950	1,013,871	189,122	28,962	160,160	100.0	15.3	84.7
1951	1,202,993	201,399	34,540	166,859	100.0	17.2	82.8
1952	1,404,392	45,825	35,139	10,686	100.0	76.7	23.3
1953	1,450,217	33,424	34,952	−1,528	100.0	104.6	−4.6
1954	1,483,641	42,368	31,316	11,052	100.0	73.9	26.1
1955	1,526,009	64,510	33,346	31,164	100.0	51.7	48.3
1956	1,590,519	76,936	33,135	43,801	100.0	43.1	56.9
1957	1,667,455	95,286	34,173	61,113	100.0	35.9	64.1
1958	1,762,741	47,407	32,854	14,553	100.0	69.3	30.7
1959	1,810,148	48,693	33,993	14,700	100.0	69.8	30.2
1960	1,858,841	52,348	35,065	17,283	100.0	67.0	33.0
1961	1,911,189						
Census: 1961	1,932,357						

Source: *Statistical Abstract of Israel, 1962*, No. 13, Section B, Table 2, p. 32, Jerusalem, 1962.

mass immigration period. During the summer of 1949, and continuing until the summer of 1950, almost the whole of the Jewish community of Yemen, some 40,000 persons, was flown to Israel during the famous "Operation Magic Carpet." In the same period most of the Jewish population of Libya was transferred to Israel, and in the following year, 1950/51, some 124,000 Jews from Iraq and 27,000 Jews from Persia immigrated to Israel in what was called "Operation Ezra and Nehemiah."

The mass immigration of 1948-1951 included for the first time a very large proportion of Jews from non-Western countries, and this immigration changed the character of the Jewish population of Israel considerably. Of the total number of Jewish immigrants in this period, no less than thirty-five percent were Jews from Asian countries (mostly Iraq, Yemen, Persia, and Turkey), and fourteen percent were from African countries (mostly Morocco, Tunisia, Algeria, and Libya). Only half, fifty-one percent, came from European or American countries, compared to ninety percent from these countries among the immigrants of the Mandatory Period. At the end of 1951, of a total Jewish population of 1,404,000, those born abroad constituted seventy-five percent of the population. Of those born abroad, thirty-seven percent were of Asian or African origin, compared to sixty-three percent of European or American origin.

Jewish immigration to Israel in 1952 and 1953 dropped to a small fraction of the numbers arriving during the mass immigration of the previous four years, with less than 36,000 immigrants arriving in the two years. There were several reasons for this reduction in the magnitude of the immigration. Potential immigrants among European Jewry had either all migrated to Israel already or were prevented from doing so by restrictions placed upon the emigration of Jews by governments of the "Iron Curtain" countries. Potential immigrants from Asian and African countries on one hand often postponed immigration due to economic difficulties in Israel and, on the other hand, were affected by a new policy of selectivity in availablity of financial aid to immigrants. Because of the many difficulties in the absorption of immigrants in Israel's first years, the latter policy assigned first priority for receipt of aid to Jews facing problems of physical security in their countries of residence and wishing to immigrate to Israel. Next priority was assigned to potentially productive workers and their families, and lowest priority for receipt of aid in immigration was given persons who, in Israel, would obviously become economic burdens upon the rest of the community.

Of the immigrants in this two-year period, 1952-1953, some twenty-nine percent were of European, American, and Oceanic birth; twenty-eight percent were of Asian origin; and forty-two percent were of African origin. The European immigrants came mostly from Rumania, although a few were of Polish and Bulgarian origin. Those of Asian origin came mostly from Persia and Iraq, while those from Africa came primarily from Tunisia and Morocco, with a few arriving from Libya.

In 1952 natural increase was a greater factor in the growth of the population than was the net migration; and in 1953 the number of Jewish emigrants from Israel exceeded the number of immigrants. Nevertheless the population continued to grow and at the end of 1953 the Jewish population of Israel was 1,484,000, including twenty-nine percent Israel-born compared to seventy-one percent foreign-born. Of those born abroad, sixty-two percent were of European, American, or Oceanic origin, twenty-eight percent were born in Asian countries, and ten percent were born in African countries.

In the period 1954-1957 immigration again began to increase, the numbers of immigrants reaching 18,370 in 1954; 37,478 in 1955; 56,234 in 1956; and 71,224 in 1957, so that a total of 183,306 Jewish immigrants arrived in Israel in that four-year period. In 1954, evidently as a reaction both to political upheavals in French North Africa (often accompanied by anti-Jewish demonstrations) and to the improvement of economic conditions in Israel, immigration of Jews from that area increased to close to 12,000 and continued to increase throughout the next three years. In addition, large numbers of Jews were expelled from Egypt following the Sinai campaign of October, 1956, and eventually found their way to Israel. In the period 1954-1957 some 114,000 Jews born in African countries immigrated to Israel and constituted sixty-three percent of the total immigration in that period.

In 1954 and 1955 immigration from European and Asian countries remained very low with the only large group from any single country being a group of 1,500 Indian Jews. In 1956 immigration from Asian countries remained at a low level, with only 3,200 immigrants arriving from Asia, mostly from Turkey and Persia. However, a sudden rise in immigration from Europe began when Poland, and, to a degree, Hungary lifted restrictions previously imposed upon Jewish emigration; and in that year 8,000 European Jewish immigrants arrived in Israel, mostly from those two countries. This immigration continued through the following year, and in 1957 some 42,000 European Jews immigrated to Israel, mostly from Poland and Hungary, but with a few from the Soviet Union.

In the period 1958-1960 a total of some 72,400 immigrants arrived in Israel, including about sixty-four percent from Europe, America, and Oceania, and about thirty-six percent from Asia and Africa. In the same period an excess of 11,200 tourists and visitors arriving was recorded over the number departing, and an excess of some 37,000 residents departing from Israel was recorded over the number arriving. Accordingly, in the period 1958-60 the Jewish population grew by some 46,500 due to the net migration.

Thus, in a period of less than thirteen years, between May 14, 1948, and December 31, 1960, a total of 981,000 Jewish immigrants arrived in Israel, more than double the number of immigrants arriving during twenty-nine years of the British Administration in Palestine from 1919 to 1948. The immigrants came from more than forty countries, from every continent on the globe, and included fifty-three percent from Europe, North and South America, and Oceania, and forty-seven percent from Asia and Africa. In this period the average annual crude birth rate was 28.5 per thousand population, and the average annual crude death rate was only 6.2 per thousand, so that the crude rate of natural increase averaged 22.3 per thousand in the period. The Jewish population of Israel thus grew by 392,000 in the 1948-1960 period due to excess of births over deaths. In all the population grew from 649,000 to 1,911,000 in the period, an increase of 194 percent, of which sixty-nine percent was due to net migration and thirty-one percent was due to natural increase. The number of children under ten years of age almost quadrupled, the Jewish population of Asian birth increased five-fold, and that of African birth increased fifteen-fold. Substantial previously unsettled areas of Israel were populated, the number of settlements more than doubled, and the rural population almost quadrupled. In common with other countries of immigration, Israel witnessed a backflow of emigrants, and in the same period, some 129,000 residents emigrated from Israel, less than seven percent of the total number of immigrants.

IV. URBAN GROWTH AND RURAL SETTLEMENT

The spectacular growth of the Jewish population of Israel that took place in the existing urban and rural places of Jewish settlement was accompanied by the no less spectacular growth of the number of places of settlement and by the expansion of Jewish settlement in Israel to areas previously uninhabited by Jews. The changing distribution of Jewish settlement is Israel, by subdistricts, is shown in Table 2.4, and the distribution of the Jewish population by roughly equivalent subdistricts in the Mandatory Government administration is given for 1944/45.

In 1944/45, about eighty-four percent of the Jewish popu-

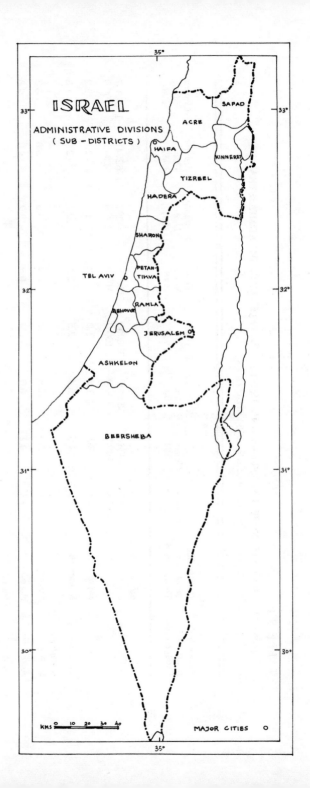

TABLE 2.4.

JEWISH POPULATION OF PALESTINE AND ISRAEL: DISTRIBUTION BY ADMINISTRATIVE SUBDISTRICTS, 1922-1961 (PERCENT DISTRIBUTION)

SUBDISTRICTS		Census 1922	Census 1931	Estimate Dec. 1944	Estimate Dec. 1945	Registration Nov. 1948	Estimate Dec. 1951	Estimate Dec. 1957	Census May 1961
Pre-Independence Designation	Post-Independence Designation								
All Palestine	All Israel	83794 100.0	174610 100.0	553600 100.0	592000 100.0	716678 100.0	1404392 100.0	1762741 100.0	1932357 100.0
Safad	Safad	4.6	2.1	1.2	1.2	1.3	1.7	2.1	2.2
Tiberias	Kinnereth	7.4	4.5	2.4	2.5	2.1	2.1	2.0	1.8
Nazareth Beisan	Jezreel	1.7	2.9	2.6	2.7	3.4	4.5	3.6	3.5
Acre	Acre	0.2	0.2	0.5	0.5	0.8	2.2	2.6	2.6
Haifa	Haifa Hadera	10.4	13.4	18.9	19.0	21.1	18.9	17.2	16.7

Tulkarm	*Sharon Petah-Tikvah*	(a)	0.4	2.7	2.9	10.4	11.8	11.6	11.2
Ramle	*Ramle Rehovoth*	4.7	4.9	5.3	5.3	4.8	9.7	9.2	8.5
Jaffa	Tel Aviv	28.8	40.0	47.8	48.3	43.2	34.8	35.0	35.8
Jerusalem	Jerusalem	41.2	31.3	18.1	17.0	12.0	10.7	9.7	9.7
Gaza Hebron	*Ashkelon*	0.9	0.3	0.5	0.6	0.7	2.0	3.6	3.9
Beersheba	Beersheba	0.1	(a)	(a)	(a)	0.2	1.6	3.4	4.1

a. Less than 1%

Source: 1922, 1931—*Survey of Palestine*, Vol. I, Table 7c, p. 149; 1944—Government of Palestine, *Statistical Abstract of Palestine*, 1944–45, Table 11, p. 22; 1945—Jewish Agency, *Statistical Handbook of Jewish Palestine, 1947* (Jerusalem, 1947) p. 40; 1948, 1961—Israel Population Census, 1961, *Demographic Characteristics of the Population*, Part I, Table 17, pp. 40–41; 1951, 1957—*Statistical Abstract of Israel, 1962*, Part B, Table 6, p. 38.

lation was concentrated in the Jaffa (Tel Aviv), Haifa, and Jerusalem subdistricts, with only two percent in the northern subdistricts of Northern and Western Galilee, Safad, and Acre, and less than one percent in the two southern subdistricts of Gaza (Ashkelon) and Beersheba. By 1961 almost five percent of the Jewish population lived in the Safad and Acre subdistricts (2.2% and 2.6%), and eight percent lived in the southern subdistricts of Ashkelon (3.9%) and Beersheba (4.1%). In 1945 there were a total of 293 places of Jewish settlement, including twenty-seven urban places and 266 rural settlements. By 1961 the number of places of settlement increased to 771, including sixty-three urban places and 708 rural settlements. At the extremities of the country there were, in 1945, only thirty Jewish places of settlement in the Acre and Safad subdistricts comprising some 10,000 persons; fourteen settlements in the Gaza (Ashkelon) subdistrict including 3,800 Jewish settlers; and only three settlements, totaling 100 persons, in the entire Beersheba (Negev) subdistrict. By 1961 there were 101 places of Jewish settlements, with an estimated population of 92,274 in the Acre and Safad subdistricts, ninety-six settlements with 76,358 inhabitants in the Ashkelon subdistrict, and seventy-three places of settlement, including 78,926 Jewish inhabitants, in the Beersheba subdistrict. Thus in 1961 almost thirteen percent of the population, over 247,000 persons, lived in areas which only fifteen years earlier were virtually uninhabited by Jews; and the major characteristic common to almost all activities, institutions, population groups, neighborhoods, and social institutions in these areas is that they simply had not existed only a few years earlier.

The Jewish population of pre-independence Palestine was distributed in six characteristic types of settlement—three urban and three rural types—and the distribution by type of settlement, as well as the types of settlement themselves, have undergone certain important changes in the course of Israel's rapid development and population growth. Three types of urban residence are distinguishable: residence in one of the three large cities—Jerusalem, Haifa, or Tel Aviv; residence in a smaller municipality; and residence in an "urban settlement" or "urban village," ordinarily not a municipality and usually a suburb of one of the large cities. The three major types of rural settlement are: villages of private farmer-entrepreneur families; smallholder settlements comprising individual family-operated farms, but organized for cooperative purchasing and marketing (*moshav*; plural—*moshavim*); and the famous collective settlements (*kibbutz*; plural—*kibbutzim*; or *kvutza*; plural—*kvutzot*) where property is owned collectively and production and consumption are organized communally.

The changes in the distribution of the Jewish population by type of settlement from 1945 through 1957 are summarized in Table 2.5. The last column of the table gives the distribution in 1961, and is based upon the new type-of-settlement classification employed after 1957. The important features of Table 2.5 include: 1. the relative growth of the rural population, from fifteen percent in 1945 to 22.5 percent at the end of 1957; 2. the growth and decline of immigrant reception centers and independent *ma'abaroth,* the temporary immigrant settlements; 3. urban growth outside the three large cities, reflecting (*a*) metropolitanization of the Tel Aviv and Haifa areas, and (*b*) the phenomenal growth of newly founded cities and of towns previously uninhabited by Jews; 4. the relative growth of the population of the cooperative smallholders' settlements (*moshavim*); and 5. the relative decline of the population of the collective settlements (*kibbutzim* and *kvutzot*).

The first immigrants arriving in the post-independence period were to a large extent housed in quarters abandoned by Arab families who left Palestine just prior to the 1948 hostilities. By the end of 1949 the number of immigrant families overtook the number of available housing units, and some 84,000 persons remained in three immigrant reception centers awaiting housing arrangements. Temporary tent villages (and later wooden- or metal-hut villages) called

TABLE 2.5.

JEWISH POPULATION OF PALESTINE, 1945, AND OF ISRAEL, 1948-1957: PERCENTAGE DISTRIBUTION BY TYPE OF SETTLEMENT

TYPE OF SETTLEMENT	1945	1948	1949	1950	1951	1952	1953	1954	1955	1956	1957	1961
Total	100.0	100.0	100.0	100.0	100.0	100.0	100.0	100.0	100.0	100.0	100.0	100.0
All Urban	84.6	83.9	75.8	78.0	76.0	76.8	76.3	76.1	76.4	77.0	77.3	84.6
Cities	64.3		59.2	65.3	63.5	65.1	65.1	64.5	63.9	64.2	63.6	69.7
Urban Settlements	20.3		9.8	5.7	4.6	5.2	5.2	5.6	6.6	6.9	7.9	14.9
Other Urban			6.8	7.0	7.9	6.5	6.0	6.0	5.9	5.9	5.8	
All Rural	15.4	16.1	15.9	18.6	22.1	22.8	23.3	23.6	23.3	22.8	22.5	15.4
Private Villages	3.2	3.5	3.0	3.6	3.1	3.2	3.9	4.0	3.7	3.6	3.6	4.5
Smallholders' Settlements (Moshavim)	5.2	4.4	4.8	6.1	6.4	7.3	6.8	7.3	7.4	7.7	7.9	6.4

Collective Settlements (Kibbutzim)	6.3	7.9	6.2	5.5	4.8	4.8	4.9	5.0	4.9	4.8	4.5	4.0
Independent Immigrant Transit Centers (Maabarot)	–	–	–	1.2	5.3	5.1	4.3	2.3	1.9	1.6	1.4	0.1
Other Rural	0.6	0.3	1.9	2.2	2.5	2.4	3.4	5.0	5.4	5.1	5.1	0.3
Immigrant Reception Centers	–	–	8.3	3.4	1.9	0.4	0.4	0.3	0.3	0.2	0.2	–

Source: 1945—Jewish Agency, *Statistical Handbook of Jewish Palestine, 1947*; 1948-57—Israel Central Bureau of Statistics, *Monthly Statistical Bulletin*, A., Vol. 10, No. 6, 1959, Table 7, pp. 246-247; 1961—Israel Census of Population, 1961, *Demographic Characteristics of the Population, Part I*, Table 34, pp. 84-85. The official "Type of Settlement" classification was changed prior to the 1961 Census, the main difference being the inclusion of certain places previously "Other Rural" in the classification "Other Urban" and certain previously "Urban Settlements" in the "Cities" classification.

45

ma'abarot (singular—*ma'abarah*) were set up to house immigrants; in these villages medical care and educational facilities were provided, and employment was sought for the men in nearby towns and villages. Some of the *ma'abarot* were administratively attached to cities, but others were administered by the Jewish Agency, the institution charged with organizing immigration and absorption of immigrants, independently of other local authorities. The combined population of independent *ma'abarot* and immigrant reception centers reached a peak of 101,000 at the end of 1951 and declined thereafter. The population of independent *ma'abarot* did, in the earliest years of independence, represent the major component of increase in the rural population. But this was more than simply a "paper increase" implied by the classification since workers from these *ma'abarot* were, in large measure, employed in agriculture and in rural villages. These *ma'abarot* were more or less replaced by the "other rural" villages, where the *ma'abarah* populations obtained permanent housing and remained in the rural population. Thus after 1951, the decline of the independent *ma'abarah* population coincided with the complementary increase in the "other rural" village population. At the same time large numbers of immigrants were settled in or near established rural villages, though part of the growth of these established rural villages is obscured by the fact that some became "urban settlements" during the period. Finally, large numbers of new immigrants were encouraged to settle in newly established *moshavim,* the cooperative smallholder settlements, and these grew in number from 104 in November, 1948, to 366 at the close of 1959. The population of these settlements increased from 30,000 to 124,000 in the same period.

The growth of the populations of the Tel Aviv and Haifa subdistricts, of the cities of Tel Aviv and Haifa, and of the "ring" populations, i.e., the populations of the subdistricts outside the cities of Tel Aviv and Haifa, is indicated in Table 2.6. Despite the fact that both the Tel Aviv and Haifa populations grew by annexation, it is readily seen that the

TABLE 2.6.

GROWTH OF TEL AVIV AND HAIFA SUBDISTRICTS, CITIES, AND "SUBURBAN RINGS," 1948-1961

	NOVEMBER, 1948	MAY, 1961	ABSOLUTE GROWTH	PERCENT INCREASE
Tel Aviv Subdistrict	305,650	699,289	393,639	123
City of Tel Aviv	248,261	386,070	137,809	52
Tel Aviv "Ring"	57,389	313,219	255,830	446
Haifa Subdistrict	125,519	276,213	150,694	115
City of Haifa	97,544	183,021	85,477	84
Haifa "Ring"	27,975	93,192	65,217	233

Source: Israel Census of Population, 1961, *Demographic Characteristics of the Population, Part I,* Tables 16, 34, pp. 38-39; 84-85.

relative growth of the "ring" populations substantially exceeded that of the cities. The table understates the extent of "metropolitan growth" in the Tel Aviv areas, as the growth of the Petach-Tikva, Ramle, and Rehovoth subdistricts (from 85,381 in November, 1948, to 304,522 in 1959) is closely associated with that of the Tel Aviv area. A considerable increase in the population of the Haifa subdistrict took place in what were in 1948 suburbs of Haifa, mostly located in the Haifa Bay area, and subsequently annexed to the City of Haifa. Although there has been a certain amount of discussion and concern over administrative and traffic problems arising in connection with these metropolitanization trends, very little attention has thus far been paid to social implications of these trends.

The growth of Jerusalem and its environs has not taken the character of metropolitanization, although the boundaries of the municipality have expanded considerably. There have been and remain substantial areas of unoccupied land within the city. Land surrounding the city is largely unsettled, being unsuited for agricultural settlement except at great cost of terracing, rock clearance, etc. Aside from a very few agricultural settlements, there is virtually no economic activity in the area outside the City of Jerusalem. Provision of water, electricity, and other services independently of the Jerusalem municipality is, at best, an extremely difficult undertaking in the rocky Judean Hills; thus expansion of settlement in Jerusalem has taken place largely in the city or in areas annexed by the city.

Some important changes have taken place in Jerusalem itself. In the first place the Jewish population of the Old City of Jerusalem (now in Jordan and inaccessible to Israeli Jews) was transferred in 1948 to the New City, and with the extension of medical, educational, and welfare services of the City of Jerusalem and of the national government this population has been integrated into the social and economic life of the new Jewish community in Israel to a far greater extent than was ever the case during the Mandate. Similarly, parts of the Jewish community in the New City of Jerusalem which, prior to independence, had been largely cut off from the affairs of the *Yishuv* are much more integrated in the schools, the army, the labor force, the religious institutions, and the welfare institutions of Israel. A very large number of Oriental immigrants have settled in Jerusalem since independence, and their integration has taken place jointly with the integration of Oriental and of some European religious communities of veteran settlers.

Secondly, the activities of the Government have been transferred to Jerusalem and these, together with the increased size and activities of the Hebrew University and of institutions such as the Jewish Agency, the Jewish National Fund, etc., all located in Jerusalem, have made that city the place of residence of relatively large numbers of professional, managerial, and clerical workers. Finally, the rapid development of tourism has generated new employment in Jerusalem and has promoted construction, public works, and retail trade in a city to some extent cut off geographically from the rest of the country and struggling to establish an economic base.

Outside the three large cities and their environs the growth of entirely new towns has been one of the most notable features of the settlement of new immigrants in Israel. In Table 2.7 the growth of six new towns—having no Jewish population at all in 1948 but totaling 131,000 Jewish residents in May 1961—and of seven towns having 19,000 Jewish residents in 1948 and 127,000 in 1961 is shown. The entirely

TABLE 2.7.

POPULATION OF TOWNS INHABITED MAINLY BY NEW JEWISH IMMIGRANTS: 1948-1961

TOWN	NOV., 1948	DEC., 1952	DEC., 1957	DEC., 1959	MAY, 1961
Ashkelon	....	12,500	21,000	22,700	24,310
Beersheba	....	14,500	32,000	39,500	43,516
Beth Shaan (Beisan)	....	3,660	9,250	10,500	9,719
Beth Shemesh	....	2,680	5,370	6,500	6,986
Dimona	....	....	2,650	4,050	5,000
Elath	....	275	2,200	4,500	5,326
Kiryath Gath	....	....	4,400	7,800	10,111
Kiryath Shmoneh	....	7,000	9,600	10,800	11,796
Rosh Ha'ayn	....	7,000	8,000	9,300	9,256
Sakhnin	....	3,769	4,500	4,900	5,150
Sub-Total	....	51,384	98,970	120,550	131,170
Acre	4,016	16,680	21,400	24,000	25,222
Afula	2,505	9,600	12,900	14,250	13,844
Lod (Lydda)	1,056	15,940	18,600	20,100	19,012
Nahariya	1,722	9,000	13,000	15,500	14,574
Ramle	1,547	19,421	23,300	23,000	22,852
Safad	2,317	7,750	9,600	10,300	10,710
Tiberias	5,566	16,200	19,600	20,750	20,792
Sub-Total	18,729	94,591	117,800	127,900	127,006
Grand Total	18,729	145,975	216,770	248,450	258,176

Source: *Statistical Abstract of Israel, 1962,* No. 13, Part B, Table 9, p. 43.

new towns (top panel) and the older towns of Lod, Ramle, and Acre are comprised almost entirely of new immigrants; and the overwhelming majority of the residents of Afula, Safad, Tiberias, and Nahariya are also new immigrants. Of the total urban growth between 1948 and 1961, some twenty-two percent was accounted for by the growth of seventeen towns apart from the three large cities—settled primarily by new immigrants—which either did not exist or had had virtually no Jewish inhabitants in 1948.

The most important organized sectors of the rural economy in Israel comprise the *kibbutzim* and *kvutzot* (the collective settlements) and the *moshavim* (the smallholders' cooperative settlements). The relative decline of the collective settlements and the growth of the smallholders' cooperative settlements (Table 2.5) have been among the most carefully noted trends in post-independence Israel. Prior to independence, the rural settlers were considered the Zionist vanguard in the *Yishuv*. Representatives of the *kibbutz* and the *moshav* organizations and movements always were—and still remain —disproportionately articulate in the pre-State Zionist activities and in post-independence Israeli politics.

The post-independence growth of the number of *moshavim* (the cooperative smallholders' settlements), and of the population of the *moshavim* is best understood as the outcome of a program designed to absorb Oriental immigrant families and to settle relatively unpopulated areas. Although the program enjoyed powerful support from the long-standing Zionist back-to-the-soil ideology, it was less a measure calculated to expand the agricultural sector of Israel's economy than it was to absorb families whose heads would otherwise have had to seek more or less casual employment in the already over-crowded market for unskilled labor. Tens of thousands of immigrant families, mostly from Asia and Africa, were settled in small communities whose relationships with the country and its social, political, and economic institutions were fixed— or at least bounded—by the rules and economic relationships governing *moshavim* and which had evolved outside any particular new settlement. In return for abiding by the rules, which had evolved in the previous growth of the *moshavim* but were constantly being altered in one or another respect by situations and social systems outside individual settlements, the immigrant families received housing and were more or less 'assured of minimal incomes—meager as they may have been—regardless of the market for their products. The latter was assured by elaborate loan and subsidization policies of the Government, the Jewish Agency, and the marketing cooperatives.

It is important to note that the *moshav qua* institution is indifferent to the primary-level social relationships obtaining in individual settlements and in individual households. Relationships between men and their families, between women and their grocers and butchers, between families, and between generations are matters of indifference to the *moshav* economic and political organizations. The latter define the individual's economic relationships to the community and the community's relationships to the national economy, to the Jewish Agency and to the Government. The Jewish Agency was the initiator and financier of the program. The Government obliged the rest of the country to underwrite the program above and beyond the Jewish Agency's participation by manipulation of prices of agricultural commodities. Thus ethnically homogeneous immigrant communities were able to organize internal and family affairs as they pleased, and individuals in such communities were relatively free of the pressures confronting new immigrants in the cities or in heterogeneous settlements. On the other hand such communities were segregated from the events and relationships of the larger Israel community. Economic and social relationships with the larger society were mediated initially by officials of the *moshav* organizations and the Jewish Agency, and later by sons and daughters serving in the army or employed outside the community, and by community members increasingly replacing the outside officials and personnel.

From November, 1948, until May 1961, a period in which

the Jewish population grew by almost 170 percent, the population of the collective settlements grew by less than forty percent, from 54,000 to 77,000. In this period the collective settlement population grew hardly beyond the growth implied by its own crude rate of natural increase. The failure of the *kibbutz* movement to grow is usually interpreted as a "decline," and collective settlements are often said to be undergoing a "crisis." The *kibbutz* is ordinarily viewed as a social movement, and a revolutionary one at that. The post-independence "decline" and "crisis" of the *kibbutz* movement is typically analyzed in terms of the relationship between the *kibbutz* ideology and the decline of the so-called "pioneering climate" in Palestine and Israel. The *kibbutz'* greatest period of expansion was in the years 1938-1947, and it seems appropriate to compare the recruitment situation in these years with that in the post-independence years.

It is important, first of all, to bear in mind that, in contrast to the *moshav*, the *kibbutz* is emphatically *not* indifferent to the primary-level social relationships of its members. The *kibbutz* claims priority in the relationship between members and the collective, and it claims the right to control many kinds of primary-level relationships. Thus *kibbutz* families have no resources to allocate to their members; the *kibbutz* allocates resources to each individual member. The *kibbutz* family has only limited control over the socialization, activities, and education of its children, the *kibbutz* itself claiming authority in these spheres, and so forth.[3]

Although families were formed in *kibbutzim*, the *kibbutz* never *attracted* any substantial numbers of family units, recruitment being concentrated primarily among unattached persons. Moreover, the *kibbutz* never attracted any substantial number of Oriental immigrants of *any* age or any marital or family status, and it never attracted Palestine-born youths of the Oriental communities. Thus recruitment to the

3. Y. Talmon-Garber, "Social Structure and Family Size," *Human Relations XII*, No. 2 (1959); and M. Spiro, *Kibbutz: Venture in Utopia* (Cambridge: Harvard University Press, 1956).

ranks of the *kibbutz* movement and of *kibbutzim* was always limited essentially to single persons either of European or Palestinean birth, but European parentage. It is possible to compute some crude estimates of the population from which the *kibbutzim* were able to attract and recruit members in the period 1939-1948 and in the period 1949-1952. When such estimates are computed, it is clear that the *number* of potential recruits hardly changed relative to the 1939-48 period. However, the ranks of European bachelor and spinster immigrants were rapidly depleted by a marriage boom in the years 1949-1952. In addition the number of occupational, career, etc., directions available to Palestinean-born youth and to European-born youth immigrating prior to independence increased very rapidly in the same period. Thus, it seems surprising that the population of the collective settlements grew in the period as much as it did.

V. VETERAN SETTLERS AND NEW IMMIGRANTS: COMPARISON OF SELECTED DEMOGRAPHIC AND SOCIO-ECONOMIC CHARACTERISTICS

The review of the growth of the Jewish population of pre-independence Palestine and of the magnitude and sources of the Jewish immigration to Israel in its first years of independence was presented to indicate, in part, the background of the problem of absorption of immigrants.

A spectacular change in the composition of Jewish immigration by geocultural origin took place in the first years of Israel's independence. Whereas almost ninety percent of the pre-independence immigrants were of European origin, in the first years of independence almost half the Jewish immigrants to Israel came from countries in Asia and Africa, mostly from Middle Eastern countries of Islamic cultures (Table 2.8). As a consequence, the composition of the Jewish population of Israel by geocultural origin changed both very rapidly and very radically (Table 2.9).

TABLE 2.8.

JEWISH IMMIGRANTS TO PALESTINE AND ISRAEL BY CONTINENT OF BIRTH, 1919-MAY, 1961, NUMBER AND PERCENT DISTRIBUTION

| CONTINENT OF BIRTH | 1919-MAY, 1948 | | MAY, 1948-MAY, 1961 | | | | | | | | |
| | | | Total | | 1948-1951 | | 1952-1954 | | 1955-1961 | |
	No.	%	No.	%	No.	%	No.	%	No.	%
Total	452,158	100.0	981,589	100.0	684,201	100.0	51,193	100.0	246,195	100.0
Europe and America	385,066	89.6	450,127	46.8	334,971	50.3	11,187	21.9	103,969	42.3
Asia and Africa	44,809	10.4	512,034	53.2	330,456	49.7	39,978	78.1	141,600	52.7
Unknown	22,283		19,428		18,774		28		626	

Source: Israel Census of Population, 1961, *Demographic Characteristics, Part I*, Introduction, Chap. 3, pp. xx-xxi.

TABLE 2.9.

JEWISH POPULATION OF ISRAEL: DISTRIBUTION BY
CONTINENT OF BIRTH, 1948-1960

PLACE OF BIRTH	NOV., 1948	DEC., 1951	DEC., 1957	DEC., 1960
Total—All Places	100.0	100.0	100.0	100.0
Israel	35.4	25.2	33.4	37.1
Asia	8.1	20.6	16.8	15.9
Africa	1.7	7.0	12.4	11.9
Europe and America	54.8	47.2	37.4	35.1

Source: *Statistical Abstract of Israel, 1962*, No. 13, Part B, Table 16, p. 51.

The European-born population comprised almost fifty-five percent of the population in 1948; by the end of 1960 it represented only thirty-five percent of the population; and the population born in Asia and Africa, comprising less than ten percent of the total in 1948, was more than one-fourth of the total Jewish population by 1951.

In this section data are summarized to indicate, at least in first approximation, some of the differences between characteristics of the veteran population of the *Yishuv* and the immigrant groups arriving in Israel during the first years of independence.

Age

The age structure of the Jewish population of Israel was not radically altered as a result of the mass immigration in the first years of independence. In Table 2.10 it is seen that the age distribution of immigrants arriving in 1948-52 was remarkably similar to that of the Jewish population of Palestine in 1945 and of Israel in November 1948 (some 100,000 immigrants had already arrived between May and November, 1948). Only percentages of immigrants aged fifteen to twenty-

TABLE 2.10.

AGE DISTRIBUTIONS (PERCENT) OF JEWISH IMMIGRANTS TO PALESTINE, 1928-1948; OF JEWISH POPULATION OF ISRAEL, NOVEMBER, 1948; OF JEWISH IMMIGRANTS TO ISRAEL, 1948-1952; AND OF JEWISH POPULATION OF ISRAEL, DECEMBER, 1952, AND MAY, 1961

	TOTAL	0-4	5-14	15-19	20-29	30-44	45-64	65+
Immigrants, 1928-1948[a]	100.0	5.4	12.3	14.7	31.9	20.1	15.6	
Jewish Population November, 1948[b]	100.0	12.0	16.6	8.4	18.0	26.0	15.1	3.9
Immigrants, 1948-1952[c]								
Total	100.0	11.7	16.7	9.7	19.6	21.1	16.9	4.3
Born in Europe-America	100.0	10.4	9.3	6.5	20.4	26.3	21.8	5.3
Born in Asia-Africa	100.0	13.0	24.5	13.0	18.7	15.6	12.0	3.2
Jewish Population:								
December, 1952[d]	100.0	13.6	17.9	8.1	16.6	22.5	17.1	4.2
December, 1957[d]	100.0	12.6	22.2	7.0	14.8	26.7	12.1	4.6
December, 1959	100.0	11.8	23.1	7.1	14.2	25.9	13.1	4.8
May, 1961[e] —Total	100.0	11.1	23.6	7.9	13.3	18.8	20.0	5.3
Born in Israel	100.0	28.6	43.4	8.8	10.8	5.4	2.3	0.7
Born in Europe-America	100.0	0.3	7.0	3.4	8.2	29.1	41.6	10.4
Born in Asia-Africa	100.0	0.7	16.8	12.3	22.2	24.2	18.1	5.7

a. Source: M. Sicron, *Immigration to Israel, 1948-1953*, Table A-17, p. 11.

b. Source: *Statistical Abstract of Israel, 1962*, No. 13, Part B; Table 12, pp. 46-47.

c. Source: M. Sicron, *op. cit.*, Table A-46, p. 36.

d. Source: *Statistical Abstract of Israel, 1959/60* (No. 11) and 1962 (No. 13).

e. Source: Israel Census of Population, 1961, *Demographic Characteristics*, Part I, Table 6, pp. 16-17.

56

nine and forty-five and older were slightly higher than in the receiving population and the percentage of immigrants aged thirty to forty-four was somewhat markedly lower.

Considering separately the age distributions of the European and Oriental (Asian and African) immigrant categories, it is clear that this surprising overall similarity is a consequence of a "balancing" of the two categories. In effect, the European immigrant population was "old" and the Oriental immigrant population "young" relative to the pre-independence community. School-aged children and adolescents were very few in number among the European immigrants (15.8% in ages 5-19) but comprised more than a third (37.5%) of the Oriental immigrants. By contrast, about half the European immigrants (48.1%) were in the thirty to sixty-four age groups compared to somewhat over one-fourth (27.6%) of the Oriental immigrants in these ages.

Other considerations ignored for the moment, it seems clear that differences in absorption of the European and of the Oriental immigrants are implied by the very differences in age structure. In the first place, the two categories of immigrants placed different demands upon the different institutions, e.g., educational, medical, social welfare, etc., and had different kinds of housing requirements. Second, different areas of social participation are implied for the two categories. Finally, different allocations of incomes, and consequent differences in consumption and style of life, seem implied. The Oriental group was burdened by a staggering dependency rate of sixty-eight (i.e., 68 persons aged 0-14 and 65 and over per every 100 persons aged 15-64) compared to a rate of thirty-three for the European group.

The various institutions of the *Yishuv* and of the State were affected, aside from the increase in numbers, by very drastic changes in the composition of each age group by place of birth. In particular the schools were strongly affected. Although there were always some children in the immigration waves to the *Yishuv*, the majority of school children and adolescents in the *Yishuv* had been born in Palestine and, of those born abroad, almost all were of European birth and from small families. By 1955, of a total of 119,541 persons aged ten to fourteen, just under one-half (48.5%) were born in Israel, eleven percent were born in Europe, twenty-seven percent in Asia, and thirteen percent in Africa. Of the population aged fifteen to nineteen, only forty percent were born in Israel. But fifty-three percent of the children aged five to nine, and a full ninety-four percent of those aged zero to four had been born in Israel.

TABLE 2.11.

JEWISH POPULATION OF ISRAEL UNDER 20 YEARS OF AGE, BY AGE GROUPS AND CONTINENT OF BIRTH (PER-CENT DISTRIBUTION), 1955

| | | PLACE OF BIRTH | | |
	Total	Israel	Asia	Africa	Europe, America
Total—under 20 years	100.0	63.5	16.0	9.0	11.5
0-4	100.0	94.2	2.3	3.1	0.4
5-9	100.0	52.9	17.6	9.9	19.6
10-14	100.0	48.5	27.1	12.9	11.5
15-19	100.0	40.1	27.0	14.2	18.7

Source: *Monthly Statistical Bulletin of Israel*, Part A, Vol. 10, No. 10, Table 5, p. 498.

Marital Status

For the period of the final years of the British Mandate, it is not possible to ascertain the composition by marital status of the Jewish population. In Table 2.12 the composition by marital status of the Jewish population of Israel aged fifteen and over in November, 1948, in December, 1952, and in May, 1961, is compared with that of immigrants arriving in the post-independence period and with that of immigrants to the *Yishuv* in the years 1919-48.

On the whole the marital status of the new immigrants was similar to that of the population of Israel in November, 1948, except that the percentage married among females was somewhat lower and the percentage widowed was rather higher. For both males and females, the percentages married and ever-married among the European immigrants are higher than those among the Oriental immigrants (the opposite is, of course, true for percentages single), and this is hardly surprising in view of the differences in age composition between the two categories.

The comparison between the 1948-52 immigrants and those arriving in the 1919-1948 period is perhaps of most interest. Of males immigrating to pre-independence Palestine, almost half of those aged fifteen or over (49.1%) were single, while somewhat over a third (35.2%) of the males immigrating in 1948-52 were single. Of the women aged fifteen and over immigrating in 1919-1948, about a third (33.8%) were single, compared to only twenty-two percent among those immigrating in 1948-52. (But the Fifth *Aliyah*, from 1932-1938, was characterized by low percentages single among both males and females.) The comparison between marital status composition of immigrants to the *Yishuv* and that of new immigrants to Israel has considerable bearing upon the comparison between the veteran settler population of Israel and the new immigrants.

The marriage rate and the nuptiality-table probabilities of ever marrying were always high in the *Yishuv*.[4] The majority of male immigrants, and a large proportion of female immigrants, arrived in Palestine single and married in Palestine, having spent some period in the country prior to marriage and household and family formation. Two presumptions follow from this: 1. such persons had some social participation and acquaintance with the *Yishuv* outside their families of orientation and before embarking upon formation

4. For a detailed analysis of marriage patterns, see K. R. Gabriel, *Nuptiality and Fertility in Israel* (Jerusalem: Hebrew University Press, 1960, in Hebrew with English summary).

TABLE 2.12.

MARITAL AND FAMILY STATUS OF JEWISH IMMIGRANTS TO
PALESTINE, 1919-1948, AND TO ISRAEL, 1948-1961, AND JEWISH
POPULATION OF ISRAEL BY MARITAL STATUS, 1948, 1952, AND
1961 (PERCENT DISTRIBUTIONS)

	MARITAL STATUS				
MALES 15+	Total	S	M	W	D
Immigrants—1919-1948, Total[a]	100.0	49.1		50.9	
1948-1952, Total[a]	100.0	35.2	61.0	3.4	0.4
Born in Europe-America	100.0	28.0	67.2	4.4	0.4
Born in Asia-Africa	100.0	43.6	53.8	2.3	0.3
1952-1954[b]	100.0	40.6	55.5	3.0	0.9
1955-1957[b]	100.0	31.8	64.8	2.7	0.7
1958[b]	100.0	27.3	69.3	2.5	0.9
1959[b]	100.0	27.0	70.1	2.1	0.8
1960[b]	100.0	26.7	68.8	3.3	1.2
1961[b]	100.0	32.4	64.7	2.2	0.7
Jewish Population, Israel, 1948[c]	100.0	33.3	63.4	2.4	0.9
1952[c]	100.0	28.7	67.6	2.5	1.2
1961	100.0	26.6	70.1	2.3	1.0

FEMALES 15+					
Immigrants—1919-1948, Total[a]	100.0	33.8		66.2	
1948-1952, Total[a]	100.0	21.6	61.2	16.0	1.2
Born in Europe-America	100.0	18.4	64.0	16.3	1.3
Born in Asia-Africa	100.0	25.8	57.7	15.6	0.9
1952-1954[b]	100.0	25.0	55.4	16.6	3.0
1955-1957[b]	100.0	21.2	60.9	15.9	2.0
1958[b]	100.0	21.8	62.8	12.9	2.5
1959[b]	100.0	20.0	64.3	13.2	2.5
1960[b]	100.0	19.0	63.2	14.7	3.1
1961[b]	100.0	23.0	61.1	13.0	2.9
Jewish Population, Israel, 1948[c]	100.0	20.7	67.9	9.8	1.6
1952[c]	100.0	16.6	69.1	12.3	2.0
1961	100.0	16.8	69.7	11.4	2.1

TABLE 2.12 Cont.

FAMILY STATUS—BOTH SEXES—ALL AGES

	Total	Unattached	IN FAMILIES Head	Dependent
Immigrants—1919-1948, Total[a]	100.0	42.9	19.6	37.5
1948-1952, Total[a]	100.0	21.9	23.5	54.6
Born in Europe-America	100.0	23.8	27.2	49.0
Born in Asia-Africa	100.0	16.9	20.4	62.7
1952-1954[b]	100.0	25.2	19.2	55.6
1955-1957[b]	100.0	10.0	21.3	68.7
1958[b]	100.0	14.7	23.9	61.4
1959[b]	100.0			
1960[b]	100.0	16.4	24.6	59.0
1961[b]	100.0	12.4	24.7	62.9

a. Source: M. Sicron, *op. cit.,* Tables A-19, A-21, A-59, A-60, A-63, and A-68.

b. Source: *Statistical Abstract of Israel 1962*, No. 13, Part D, Table 7, p. 101.

c. Source: *Monthly Statistical Bulletin of Israel*, Part A, Vol. II, No. 6, June, 1960, Supplement, Table 1, p. 279 and Table 5, p. 283.

d. Source: Israel Census of Population, *Demographic Characteristics of the Population, Part I*, Table 11, pp. 26-27.

of their own families, and 2. the period spent single in the country and the fact that courtship and marriage took place in Palestine rather than abroad is of no small influence in patterns of family formation, socialization of children, consumption, and style of life, and more general orientations. By contrast, very large proportions of the new immigrants to Israel arrived already married, and it may be presumed that, at least in some respects, the character of marriage and family relationships is influenced by marriages having taken place abroad, and that social participation outside the family is affected by absence of corresponding "periods single" in Israel.

A similar contrast appears in the comparison of percentages attached and unattached to families among immigrants to the *Yishuv* and to Israel in 1948-52 (right hand panel of Table 2.12). Among immigrants of all ages to the *Yishuv*, forty-three percent arrived unattached to families and fifty-seven percent were heads of families or dependents, while among new immigrants to Israel, only twenty-two percent were unattached, twenty-three percent were heads of families, and fifty-five percent were dependents. Thus in the *Yishuv* a very large proportion of persons formed all their family ties in the country, so that family organization in the veteran population was, in considerable measure, an indigenous phenomenon despite the fact that the *Yishuv* too was largely composed of immigrants. By contrast, the family ties of new immigrants in the early years of Israel's independence were overwhelmingly ties formed abroad.

Size of Family

As was the case for marital status, it is not possible to obtain the distribution by size of families in the *Yishuv*. Indeed, the first countrywide data on size of families since the 1931 Palestine Census of Population were obtained only in June, 1954, when the Israel Central Bureau of Statistics carried out its first sample survey of the labor force.[5] In Table 2.13 the 1954 data and 1961 census are given separately for veteran settlers and new immigrants, so that some comparison of family size in the sub-populations is possible. It should be noted, however, that a marriage and baby boom affected size of family among both veteran settlers and new immigrants.[6]

In general there was a large percentage of couples without children among the new immigrants. The percentage of such couples among family units immigrating from Europe was much higher (46.1%) than among those from Asia and Africa (28.2%) but lower than among immigrants (mostly European) to the *Yishuv* (54.4%) in the Mandatory Period.

5. CBS, *Labour Force Survey, June 1954* (Jerusalem: Israel Central Bureau of Statistics, Special Series No. 56, 1957).
6. Gabriel, *op. cit.*

It is of interest to note that the percentage of childless couples (46% and 28%) among European and Oriental newly arriving immigrant families, was only 26% and 13% in the European and Oriental new immigrant populations *in Israel* in 1954, despite a very large number of marriages in both groups soon after immigration. Similarly, among the European immigrants arriving in 1948-52, there were almost no (only 1.4%) large families (six or more persons) compared to twenty-two percent of six- or more-person families among the Oriental new immigrants in 1948-52 and to six percent of large families among immigrants to the *Yishuv* in 1919-48. However the percentage of large families among the European new immigrant population in Israel was six percent in 1954, and that among the Oriental new immigrant families was no less than thirty-nine percent.

Thus the European immigrant families were, upon arrival in Israel, evidently smaller than families in the *Yishuv,* while the Oriental families were much larger. These differences had consequences for housing requirements, allocation of time, activities, and earnings, the status of women and their freedom to participate in activities outside the home, the relative attention and material goods received by children, and general relative importance of family and non-family activities and pursuits in the European and Oriental immigrant groups.

The delay in family formation inferred from the large proportion of childless couples among the European immigrants also implied that a larger proportion of children of European new immigrants would be born in Israel, and of these, a large proportion would be born to relatively older mothers having first births. Moreover a much larger proportion of families of European immigrant couples would, when complete, include all children born in Israel, while, at least in the early years after immigration, families of a large proportion of Oriental immigrant couples were bound to be mixed with respect to place of birth of the children.

TABLE 2.13.

JEWISH FAMILIES IN ISRAEL, BY AREA OF BIRTH AND PERIOD OF IMMIGRATION OF HEAD; AND
IMMIGRATING FAMILIES, 1919-1948 AND 1948-1961: PERCENT DISTRIBUTION BY SIZE

| | Total | NUMBER IN FAMILY | | | | | | | | Mean |
		2	3	4	5	6	7	8	9+	
*Immigrating Families*a										
1919-1948—Total	100.0	54.4	21.7	12.6	5.8		5.5			2.9
1948-1952—Total	100.0	38.7	28.4	15.6	7.5		9.8			3.2
1948-1952—Head Born										
in Europe, America	100.0	46.1	34.4	14.7	3.4		1.4			2.8
1948-1952—Head Born										
in Asia, Africa	100.0	28.2	19.8	16.9	13.5		21.6			3.8
1952-1954—Total	100.0	33.7	18.6	14.7	12.0		21.0			3.9
1955-1957—Total	100.0	22.7	19.7	21.1	12.6		23.9			4.2
1958-1959—Total	100.0	30.5	28.5	21.6	7.8		11.6			3.6
1960—Total	100.0	33.3	28.1	23.3	6.7		8.6			3.4
1961—Total	100.0	32.0	29.2	19.4	7.6		11.8			3.5

Families in Israel[b]

June 1954—Total	100.0	21.2	24.2	24.9	13.5	6.9	4.2	2.4	2.7	4.0
Veteran Residents:									
Head Born in Israel	100.0	19.8	23.9	25.9	14.3	6.5	4.2	2.1	3.3	4.1
" " *Europe, America*	100.0	23.9	26.5	30.0	13.6	3.9	1.2	0.5	0.4	3.6
" " *Asia, Africa*	100.0	15.3	14.1	19.8	17.3	10.9	9.2	4.8	8.6	4.9
New Immigrants:									
Head Born in *Europe, America*	100.0	26.5	31.2	26.7	10.1	3.8	0.8	0.3	0.6	3.4
" " *Asia, Africa*	100.0	13.1	15.4	16.4	15.8	14.2	11.4	7.2	6.5	5.0
Average 1961—Total	100.0	21.6	21.5	26.9	13.5	6.5	4.2	2.9	3.9	4.1

a. Source: M. Sicron, *op. cit.*, Table A-23 and Table A-81.
b. Source: Israel Central Bureau of Statistics, *Labour Force Survey, June 1954* Tables 41, 42; *Statistical Abstract of Israel 1962*, No. 13, Part B, Table 22, p. 59.

Religious Observance

The extent to which the Jewish community in Palestine and Israel was or is religious or irreligious has been the subject of much speculation, guesswork, argument, and very little systematic knowledge. As indicated above, communities of religious Jews in Palestine date from the Middle Ages, and it is usually presumed that the entire Jewish population of Palestine prior to the modern Zionist-inspired immigration was very orthodox. The anti-Zionist religious organization, the *Agudat Israel,* claimed to represent twenty percent of the Jewish population of Palestine prior to independence. Religious groups played an important part in the world Zionist movement from its very beginnings. In the *Yishuv,* the religious *Mizrahi* and *Poel Mizrahi* were Zionist political parties instrumental in organizing immigration and settlement, schools, labor and youth movements, and a variety of religious and welfare institutions all *within* the framework of the "Zionist enterprise."

In the later years of the Mandate, the non-Zionist *Agudat Israel* organization did cooperate with the Zionist parties and supported the Zionist immigration policy and some political action. Following the end of the Mandate and Israel's independence, the *Agudat Israel* accepted the legitimacy of the Jewish State (previously this organization had held that such a state may be created only by God, and not by political action of Jews) and became and has remained an active political party in Israel. A more extreme religious organization, the *Naturei Karta,* still does not accept the legitimacy of Israel's political independence or of the Israel Government.

Throughout the Mandatory Period the number of "religious" persons in the Jewish community was never actually known, and the non-religious (but not necessarily anti-religious) Zionist parties always claimed many religious adherents in their ranks. In the 1949 elections to the first Israel *Knesset* (Parliament) the religious parties polled fourteen percent of the vote.[7] All knowledge about the Oriental Jewish communities strongly suggested that these were traditional communities in many respects and, in particular, were characterized by more or less strict religious observance. As a result, it was anticipated that, in subsequent elections to the *Knesset*, the religious parties would surely gain additional support from among the Oriental immigrants. The religious parties were doomed to disappointment, and the non-religious parties were elated, when in the 1951 elections the religious parties polled only thirteen percent of the vote. In 1955 and 1959, the religious parties did make some gains, receiving fourteen percent and fifteen percent of the vote in the two elections. The actual extent of religious observance in the Jewish population of Israel remains a matter of conjecture.

Data permitting some comparison of the extent of religious observance in the veteran settler and new immigrant populations are available from a survey of maternity cases conducted in Israel in 1959/60,[8] and these are given in Table 2.14. The data must be interpreted with considerable caution. In the first place, they are derived from a sample of maternity cases so that, to the extent that fertility of religious women is greater than that of nonreligious women, the sample embodies an upward bias with respect to the percent "observant" among the women and a downward bias with respect to percent "non-observant." Assuming, however, that having at least one birth is independent of the extent of religious observance, this bias disappears for the distribution by extent of religious observance of women having first-order births.

7. CBS, *Statistical Abstract No. 11*, p. 415, and *Supra*, Table 3.1.

8. Details of the survey and procedures used are described in the preface to R. Bachi and J. Matras, *Fertility and Contraception, Summary Tables of Findings of Surveys of Jewish Maternity Cases in Israel* (Jerusalem: Hebrew University Press, mimeographed in Hebrew and English, 1961), cited hereafter as Bachi and Matras, *Summary Tables;* and a summary, in English, of the major findings of the survey is contained in R. Bachi and J. Matras, "Contraception and Induced Abortion among Jewish Maternity Cases in Israel," *Milbank Memorial Fund Quarterly*, XL., No. 2 (April, 1962).

The differences between the distributions of the sample as a whole and those of women having first- and second-order births are indicated in the top panel of Table 2.14.

On the other hand, the distributions by extent of religious observance of women in the sample having first-order births are not adequate estimates of the distribution of women in the entire Jewish population of Israel. The women having first-order births are younger, more likely to have married in Israel, more likely to have received some education, spent some of their adolescence, and served in the army in Israel than are women in the population generally; and it is likely that these distributions are downward biased with respect to percent "observant" and upward biased with respect to percent "non-observant."

In the second place, being "observant" does not necessarily mean the same thing for all persons or for all groups. The criterion for classification as "observant" was regular observance of the orthodox Jewish ritual bath tradition. For women born in Europe and Israel observance of the ritual bath tradition is almost always associated with strict adherence to all other religious prescriptions and proscriptions and, in particular, with religious regulation of marital sexual relations. But among women born in Asia and Africa observance of the ritual bath tradition may, in many instances, be independent of observance of other religious prescriptions and of religious regulation of marital sexual relations.[9]

Finally, the data refer to maternity cases in 1959/60. Of the women in the sample only twenty-four percent were married prior to 1950. Of these more than two-thirds were married in the period 1945-1949. Thus the distribution by extent of religious observance of women in the veteran settler population has reference less to married women of the *Yishuv* than to women passing through adolescence during, say, World

---

9. A more detailed discussion of the classification by religious observance is included in J. Matras and C. Auerbach, "On Rationalization of Family Formation in Israel," *Milbank Memorial Fund Quarterly*, XL, No. 4 (October, 1962), and especially in the Appendix.

War II and the last years of the Mandate and marrying only after Israel's independence. Similarly, of the new immigrants, some were adolescents or children at the time of immigration and had lived in Israel as long as eleven years prior to marriage.

With these reservations and cautions in mind, it is possible to make some comparisons of the extent of religious observance between the new immigrant and veteran settler maternity cases, and these are given in the lower panel of Table 2.14. Only twenty percent of the new immigrants reported no observance at all of religious prescriptions and admonishments, while no less than fifty-six percent reported being "observant" to the extent of adherence to the ritual bath laws and twenty-four percent (the "partially observant") reported observance of some traditions, such as Sabbath rules, dietary laws, etc., but not the ritual bath. By contrast, almost half (48.3%) of the veteran settler maternity cases reported no observance at all. But recalling both the percentages voting for a religious party in the first *Knesset* elections and the relative neglect of religious organizations and institutions in the literature dealing with the *Yishuv,* it is of interest to note that thirty-two percent of the veteran settler maternity cases reported themselves "partially observant," and almost a fifth (19.4%) indicated full adherence to orthodox precepts and "observant" to the extent of following the ritual bath tradition.

Among the veteran settler women of Asian and African birth religious observance is substantially more common than among Israel-born or European-born veteran settlers, but much less frequent than among Oriental new immigrant women. More than two thirds (68.9%) of the Oriental new immigrants reported being "observant," compared to less than two-fifths (38.4%) of the veteran settlers of Asian and African birth; and only one-tenth (10.8%) of the new immigrants indicated non-observance, compared to almost a third (31.8%) of the veteran settlers. European new immigrant women reported non-observance to about the same extent as

TABLE 2.14.

RELIGIOUS OBSERVANCE OF JEWISH MATERNITY CASES IN ISRAEL, 1959-60, BY CONTINENT OF BIRTH AND ORDER OF PRESENT BIRTH; AND BY PERIOD OF IMMIGRATION (PERCENT DISTRIBU-TION)[a]

PLACE OF BIRTH, BIRTH ORDER, AND PERIOD OF IMMIGRATION		EXTENT OF RELIGIOUS OBSERVANCE			
	Total	Non-Observant	Partially Observant	Observant	N[b]
All Periods of Immigration:					
All Maternity Cases	100.0	27.5	26.2	46.3	2973
First Births	100.0	41.0	32.0	27.0	822
Born in Israel—Total	100.0	49.2	34.2	16.6	648
First Births	100.0	56.6	30.7	12.7	255
Second Births	100.0	48.1	40.9	11.0	199
Born in Europe, America—					
Total	100.0	49.2	33.4	17.4	749
First Births	100.0	57.4	34.6	8.0	224
Second Births	100.0	53.7	35.0	11.3	275

Born in Asia, Africa—				
Total	100.0	12.2	20.9	66.9	1576
First Births	100.0	20.0	31.2	48.8	343
Second Births	100.0	16.5	22.3	61.2	314
Veteran Residents—Total	100.0	48.3	32.3	19.4	1019
Born in Israel	100.0	49.2	34.2	16.6	648
Born in Europe, America	100.0	48.8	29.7	21.5	220
Born in Asia, Africa	100.0	31.8	29.8	38.4	151
New Immigrants—Total	100.0	20.0	23.8	56.2	1954
Born in Europe, America	100.0	49.2	35.0	15.8	529
Born in Asia, Africa	100.0	10.8	20.3	68.9	1425

a. Source: R. Bachi and J. Matras, *Fertility and Contraception, Summary Tables of Findings of Surveys of Jewish Maternity Cases in Israel* (Jerusalem: Hebrew University Press, mimeographed in Hebrew and English, 1961) Table 5, page 6, and Table A, pp. 43-44.

b. See note in *Ibid.*, p. 6 concerning inflation of sample results.

did Israel-born and European-born veteran settlers, but reported "partial observance" slightly more frequently and "observance" slightly less frequently than did the veteran settlers.

The limitations of these data notwithstanding, it seems clear that religious observance is much more common among the Oriental new immigrant women than among any of the other broad groups of women, and it seems not unreasonable to infer that the same relationships hold for males. Moreover, the extent of religious observance in the Jewish population as a whole may be rather greater than is often supposed, as no less than fifty-nine percent of *all* women having first-order births reported themselves either "partially observant" or "observant."

One result completely free of sample bias concerns the composition (in 1959/60) of fertility by religious observance of the mothers. In the distribution for all maternity cases in Table 2.14, it is seen that forty-six percent of all births were to "observant" mothers and twenty-six percent to "partially observant" mothers. Just over one-fourth of the births (27.5%) were to mothers reporting themselves "non-observant."

The relationship between religious observance and other activities and social characteristics in Israel has barely been investigated. It seems clear from the same study of maternity cases that there is a negative relationship between religious observance and practice of family limitation[10] and, presumably, there is some positive association between religious observance and support of religious political parties, participation in religious activities and institutions, etc. But though the relationships between religious observance and such factors as leadership patterns, extrafamilial activities and allocation of leisure time, rationalistic or traditionalistic orientations, etc., have been almost unexplored in Israel, it seems likely that differences between veteran and new immigrant populations with respect to religious observance are of very

10. *Ibid.*, and Bachi and Matras, "Contraception and Induced Abortions . . . ," *loc. cit.*

great interest and relevance to problems of absorption of immigrants and of social change.

Educational Attainment

Other than tales about professors and surgeons laying aside their books and instruments to become pioneer chicken farmers and pioneer taxicab drivers, very little is known about levels of educational attainment of the Jewish population of Palestine prior to independence. Both the Jewish Agency's Department of Statistics and the Mandatory Government Statistician asserted that primary school attendance was virtually universal in the Jewish population.[11] From the available statistical data it is difficult to ascertain if this was in fact the case, and the Government Statistician made a point of noting that about twelve percent of the Jewish children aged six to twelve in Jerusalem received no education whatever. The Mandatory Government seems not to have exerted any notable effort in the promotion of education in the Jewish community, and neither the Government nor any of the Jewish institutions seems ever to have undertaken publication, if indeed collection, of data pertaining to levels of educational attainment.

Heads of families immigrating to Israel are asked on the standard immigrant registration forms to give particulars of educational background.[12] Probably due to difficulties in coding these responses, no tabulations relating to level of education of immigrant family heads has ever been published for post-independence immigrants or for immigrants to the *Yishuv*. *The Labour Force Survey* of June 1954 provided the first data relating to educational attainment of the Jewish population aged fifteen and over, and these are summarized in Table 2.15. In addition to limitations associated with the time interval since immigration (as was the case

11. Government of Palestine, *Statistical Abstract of Palestine, 1944-45, op. cit.*, p. 190; and Jewish Agency for Palestine, *Statistical Handbook of Jewish Palestine*, 1947, *op. cit.*

12. Sicron, *op. cit.* Vol. 1 (Hebrew edition), p. 13.

for marital status data in Table 2.12), the "educational attainment" referred to in the data is, more often than not, educational attainment in countries other than Israel or Palestine, and the publication originally presenting the data does not indicate how country-to-country comparability was affected.[13]

For both males and females there are notable differences between the distribution by educational attainment of veteran settlers and of new immigrants. More than half the male new immigrants (52.8%) did not complete primary education and twelve percent did not attend school at all. Of the veteran settlers, twenty-two percent did not complete primary education, but ninety-six percent attended some school for some period. Although there are more striking differences between European and Oriental immigrants within the new immigrant group (72% of the Oriental male new immigrants did not complete primary education compared to 35.7% among the European males), there are marked differences between European-born veteran settlers and new immigrants, large numbers of the latter group having been prevented by the war from completing their education. Similarly, the Oriental new immigrants are characterized by lower levels of education than those of the veteran settler population of Asian and African birth.

A similar pattern obtains for females, with the notable exception that the majority of the Oriental women, both veteran settlers and new immigrants (53.2% and 57.8%) had attended *no* school at all, and only thirteen percent of the Oriental new immigrant women had completed primary education. Thus both the European and Oriental new immigrants were relatively underprivileged in terms of educational attainment as compared to the veteran settler population. Especially the Oriental immigrants were at an obvious

13. CBS, *Standard of Education of the Population (June 1954).* (Jerusalem: Israel Central Bureau of Statistics, Special Series No. 66, 1958).

TABLE 2.15.

EDUCATIONAL ATTAINMENT (PERCENT DISTRIBUTION) OF JEWISH POPULATION AGED 15 AND OVER, BY SEX, CONTINENT OF BIRTH, AND DURATION OF RESIDENCE, ISRAEL, 1954

	Total	Did Not Attend School	Did Not Complete Primary Education	Completed Primary Education	Completed Post-Primary Education	Completed Higher Education
MALES: TOTAL (15+)	100.0	8.2	31.8	35.2	19.9	4.9
All Veteran Residents	100.0	4.1	22.3	39.6	26.8	7.2
Born in Israel	100.0	2.0	24.0	49.8	21.4	2.8
Born in Europe-America	100.0	1.0	17.7	37.7	33.4	10.2
Born in Asia-Africa	100.0	21.8	39.8	28.7	7.6	2.1
All New Immigrants	100.0	12.0	40.8	31.0	13.4	2.8
Born in Europe-America	100.0	2.6	33.1	41.2	18.3	4.8
Born in Asia-Africa	100.0	22.5	49.5	19.5	7.8	0.7
FEMALES: TOTAL (15+)	100.0	21.7	24.2	33.4	18.3	2.4
All Veteran Residents	100.0	11.8	18.5	39.9	26.1	3.7
Born in Israel	100.0	7.3	21.2	48.7	20.6	2.2
Born in Europe-America	100.0	4.8	16.3	40.4	33.4	5.1
Born in Asia-Africa	100.0	53.2	23.4	18.5	4.5	0.4
All New Immigrants	100.0	30.3	29.2	27.7	11.6	1.2
Born in Europe-America	100.0	6.3	31.9	40.6	19.2	2.0
Born in Asia-Africa	100.0	57.8	26.2	13.0	2.8	0.2

Source: *Statistical Abstract of Israel 1959/60*, No. 11, Table 32, p. 394.

disadvantage in the labor market and in all social spheres demanding the skills and articulateness associated with formal education, and this disadvantage was bound to inhibit or set limits upon the changes otherwise possible with increased duration of residence in Israel.

More spectacular was the entrance into the Jewish population of really large numbers of illiterate persons, reflected in the percentages among the Oriental immigrants never attending school at all. For these persons the complete unfamiliarity with abstractions and inability to manipulate symbols necessarily rendered interaction in unfamiliar situations difficult and operated to force dependence upon the traditional and the familiar in social spheres in which tradition and experience had no real relevance.

Associations between educational attainment and other socio-economic characteristics have been well documented in Israel as elsewhere, and the great differences between educational attainment in the veteran population and in the new immigrant population are regarded at popular, academic, and official levels and spheres of opinion in Israel as the major social problem of Israel.[14]

Working Force Participation

There appear to be no studies at all of the extent of participation in the working force in the Jewish population of Palestine during the last years of the British Mandate, and even the computation of the percentage of the population gainfully employed is beset with difficulties. Both the Jewish Agency and the Mandatory Government Statistician published estimates of the number of Jews gainfully employed in 1945, so that it would seem possible to compute such a percentage for that year. As it happens, there are no less than four more or less "official" estimates of the Jewish

14. See, for example, D. Patinkin, "Introduction," in Falk Project for Economic Research in Israel, *Fifth Report, 1959-60* (Jerusalem: Falk Project for Economic Research, 1961).

population of Palestine for the end of 1945: an official estimate of the Government Statistician, 554,329; a "revised *de
facto*" estimate of the Government Statistician, 579,227; an
estimate of the Department of Statistics of the Jewish Agency,
592,000; and an estimate made after independence by the
Israel Central Bureau of Statistics, 563,829. There is a similar
variety of estimates of the Jewish population as of the close
of the year 1944, except that for 1944 the Government Food
Controller has an independent estimate which is greater, as
it happens, than all the others. The Government Statistician's
estimate of the number of Jews "gainfully employed" in 1945
is 237,500 and presumably excludes unemployed persons. The
Jewish Agency's Department of Statistics' estimate of the
number of Jewish "earners," probably intended to include
unemployed persons who are normally gainful workers, is
225,000.[15]

Depending upon which combination of estimates is
chosen for numerators and denominators, estimates of the
percent participating in the working force in the Jewish
community of Palestine during 1945 may range from thirty-
seven percent to forty-five percent. Estimates of percentages
in the working force among different subgroups or categories
of the population, while not entirely impossible to derive,
are not likely to be very accurate.

In Table 2.16, the percentages reporting gainful occupations abroad are given for the Jewish immigrants to Palestine
in the Mandatory Period and for Jewish immigrants to Israel
in the years 1950-52. The latter vary somewhat from year to
year, depending probably upon the composition of the immigration in each year by *country* of origin and by age. Males
over fifteen years old among the new immigrants are characterized by higher percentages reporting previous gainful

15. Government of Palestine, *Statistical Abstract, 1944-45, op. cit.*,
p. 16; Jewish Agency *Handbook, 1947, op. cit.*, p. 66. and p. 163;
Palestine, *Survey of Palestine, op. cit.*, Vol. I, p. 163 and Vol. II, p. 732;
and CBS, *Stat. Abstract No. 11.*, Table 2, p. 7.

TABLE 2.16.

PERCENT OF JEWISH IMMIGRANTS TO PALESTINE AND ISRAEL
REPORTING PREVIOUS GAINFUL EMPLOYMENT, BY PERIOD OF
IMMIGRATION AND BY SEX, 1919-1952[a]

| | PERCENT REPORTING PREVIOUS GAINFUL EMPLOYMENT | | | | |
| PERIOD OF IMMIGRATION | *Percent of All Immigrants* | | | *Percent of Immigrants Ages 15-65*[b] | |
	Total	Male	Female	Male	Female
1919-1923	57.0				
1924-1931	51.0				
1932-1933	46.0				
1934-1938	34.4	57.7	12.2	62.0	14.2
1939-1945	36.1	55.9	12.8	64.5	13.1
1946-1947	25.5				
1950	33.6	56.5	10.8	84.5	15.7
1951	29.1	51.6	6.9	87.4	11.0
1952	33.0	52.3	13.2	87.0	20.5
1950-1952 Immigrants:					
Born in Europe					
1950	32.8	65.9	13.8	88.9	18.1
1951	31.8	67.3	10.7	95.6	14.6
1952	46.0	73.0	25.8	100.0	33.5
Born in Asia					
1950	23.1	46.5	4.4	77.9	7.3
1951	24.4	49.5	4.0	92.3	7.0
1952	22.3	44.4	3.3	80.2	5.5
Born in Africa					
1950	31.0	52.4	13.4	84.2	22.2
1951	28.5	48.2	11.5	78.4	18.8
1952	27.8	45.2	10.3	80.8	17.9

a. Source: M. Sicron, *Immigration to Israel, 1948-52*, Vol. 2, Statistical
Supplement, Tables A-25, A-26, and A-87.

b. Percent of Immigrants age 16 or over for 1934-45.

employment than are those over sixteen years of age in the
1934-38 period, the latter group including a substantial proportion of students. Very few female new immigrants born

in Asia reported working force attachments abroad, but somewhat surprisingly high percentages of new immigrant women born in Africa did report previous gainful employment.

In Table 2.17, labor force participation (employed and at work; employed but absent from work; seeking employment during the survey week) rates in Israel in June 1954 are compared for veteran settlers and for new immigrants over fourteen years of age, using data from the first *Labour Force Survey*. The differences are most striking for women, with married women in the veteran settler population characterized by much higher rates than the new immigrants. By contrast, single women among the new immigrants have somewhat higher rates of labor force participation, reflecting a greater proportion of school attendance among single women in the veteran settler population. Of women born in Asia and Africa, *both* new immigrants and veteran settlers are characterized by low rates of labor force participation. The low rates reflect both the low levels of education and consequent limited access to employment opportunities and, apparently, traditional patterns of disapproval of employment of married women outside the home.

Among the married males, new immigrants are characterized by lower rates of labor force participation, evidently reflecting difficulties in finding employment and consequent "retirement" from the labor force, particularly at ages over 55.[16] For single men, the relationship is reversed, with a larger percentage of new immigrants than of veteran residents in the labor force reflecting, probably, greater educational opportunities for the veteran settlers.

Occupational Distribution

Both the Jewish Agency and the Mandatory Government statistical organizations made estimates of the occupational

16. Data not shown here indicate low labor force participation rates for new immigrants over 55 years of age and relatively high unemployment among persons that age in the labor force.

TABLE 2.17.

JEWISH POPULATION OF ISRAEL AGED 14+: PERCENT IN THE CIVILIAN LABOR FORCE, JUNE, 1954, BY SEX, CONTINENT OF BIRTH, DURATION OF RESIDENCE, AND BY MARITAL STATUS[a]

CONTINENT OF BIRTH AND DURATION OF RESIDENCE	Total Both Sexes	SEX AND MARITAL STATUS							
		Males				Females			
		Total	S	M	W D	Total	S	M	W D
Total 14+	49.4	76.6	53.2	87.7	49.7	21.7	41.3	16.6	22.7
Veteran Residents—Total	52.8	78.1	59.3	92.4	57.7	25.8	42.4	21.4	30.1
Born in Israel	43.5	59.1	...	...	...	27.4	...	...	...
Born in Europe-America	60.3	91.5	...	...	...	27.9	...	...	...
Born in Asia-Africa	50.2	83.2	...	...	...	15.2	...	...	...
New Immigrants—Total	46.3	75.2	67.0	85.2	41.6	18.1	46.6	12.3	18.2
Born in Europe-America	51.6	83.8	...	...	...	21.5	...	...	...
Born in Asia-Africa	43.8	74.5	...	...	...	14.8	...	...	...
ALL DURATIONS OF RESIDENCE									
Born in Israel	...	59.1	45.5	92.2	62.7	27.4	34.6	20.7	33.8
Born in Europe-America	...	87.8	75.0	91.7	52.9	24.6	56.0	20.9	27.5
Born in Asia-Africa	...	76.3	68.1	81.4	39.9	15.0	46.4	6.1	14.2

a. Source: Israel Central Bureau of Statistics, *Labour Force Survey, June, 1954*, Jerusalem, 1957, Tables 7-10.

80

structure of the Jewish working force in Palestine for 1945.[17] Both classifications of earners by occupation tend to be industrial rather than occupational classifications, and comparison with current Israel Central Bureau of Statistics labor force statistical series is difficult. Similarly, industrial classifications (different ones) were used in tabulating data on occupations abroad for immigrants arriving in 1919-48 during the Mandatory Period and after 1948.

In the first *Labour Force Survey* carried out in Israel in 1954 employed persons were asked, in addition to present occupations, their occupations abroad prior to immigration (if they were employed at all). These data on occupations abroad, and not the immigration data (the latter are summarized in considerable detail by Sicron),[18] are given in the upper panel of Table 2.18. The top two lines of Table 2.18 give the two estimates, the Mandatory Government's and the Jewish Agency's, of the occupational distribution of gainful workers in the Jewish population of Palestine in 1945 in terms of the occupational categories of the 1954 *Labour Force Survey*. It is necessary to bear in mind that the conversion to this set of categories is performed very crudely indeed, as no detailed categories are given. The rest of the table gives the occupational distributions for the total labor force by sex, and for employed persons by sex, for veteran settlers and new immigrants, and by continent of birth.

Differences with respect to occupations abroad between veteran settlers and new immigrants are apparent in the percentages reporting professional occupation abroad (14.7% among the veteran settlers compared to 6.5% among new immigrants), clerical occupations (14.9% for veterans; 11.2% for new immigrants), sales occupations (26.5% and 31.0% for veterans and new immigrants), and crafts, industrial, and building trades (30.0% among the veteran settlers and 34.5% among the new immigrants). Differences of the same nature

17. Government of Palestine, *Survey of Palestine, op. cit.*, Vol. 2, p. 732; Jewish Agency, *Handbook, 1947, op. cit.*, p. 66.
18. Sicron, *op. cit.*, Vol. I. Chapter 10.

TABLE 2.18.

JEWISH POPULATION OF ISRAEL: OCCUPATIONAL DISTRIBUTION OF PERSONS IN THE LABOR FORCE AND OF EMPLOYED PERSONS IN ISRAEL, JUNE, 1954, BY SEX, CONTINENT OF BIRTH, AND DURATION OF RESIDENCE: AND OCCUPATIONS ABROAD OF PERSONS EMPLOYED ABROAD AND IN ISRAEL

	TOTAL	PROF., TECH., & RELATED	MANAGERIAL	CLERICAL	SALES	FARMERS & UNSKILLED AGRICULTURAL	DRIVERS & TRANS., EXCLUDING UNSKILLED	CRAFTS INDUSTRIAL & BUILDING EXCLUDING UNSKILLED	SERVICE, EXCLUDING UNSKILLED	UNSKILLED
Palestine, 1945										
Government Estimates	100.0	8.4	14.2		11.0	14.8	4.2	34.2	13.2	
Jewish Agency Estimates	100.0	10.2	14.0		15.6	10.7	5.3	32.2	12.0	
Israel, 1954—										
Total Labor Force	100.0	9.9	2.7	13.1	10.0	13.9	4.1	24.2	8.4	13.7
Male	100.0	6.5	3.1	12.5	10.1	14.6	5.1	27.3	5.0	15.8
Female	100.0	22.9	1.3	15.6	9.5	11.4	(0.2)	12.6	21.0	5.5
Employed, Total	100.0	10.4	2.8	13.5	10.4	13.5	4.2	24.0	8.5	12.7
Male	100.0	6.8	3.2	12.9	10.6	14.2	5.2	27.2	5.1	14.8
Female	100.0	23.4	1.3	15.9	9.7	11.3	(0.1)	12.1	20.9	5.3

Employed, Veteran									
Residents	100.0	13.8	4.4	17.2	11.1	9.7	5.5	24.1	6.5	7.7
Male	100.0	8.9	5.1	16.3	11.4	9.6	7.1	28.3	4.3	9.0
Female	100.0	30.0	1.8	20.2	10.4	9.8	0.2	10.2	14.0	3.4
Employed, New									
Immigrants	100.0	6.5	1.0	9.5	9.6	17.8	2.7	23.9	10.7	18.3
Born in Europe-America	100.0	8.5	1.4	12.0	11.4	11.1	3.4	27.1	10.0	15.1
Born in Asia-Africa	100.0	3.4	0.4	5.9	7.1	27.4	1.5	19.5	11.8	23.0
All Origins—Male	100.0	4.6	1.1	9.4	9.7	18.9	3.3	26.1	6.1	20.8
All Origins—Female	100.0	14.6	0.6	10.1	8.8	13.2	0.0	14.7	30.3	7.7
Occupations Abroad—Total	100.0	9.2	2.6	12.4	29.5	2.3	2.3	33.0	2.6	6.1
Veteran Residents	100.0	14.7	2.8	14.9	26.5	2.9	1.7	30.0	1.5	5.0
New Immigrants	100.0	6.5	2.5	11.2	31.0	2.0	2.5	34.5	3.2	6.6
Veteran Residents plus									
New Immigrants									
Europe-America	100.0	11.6	3.2	14.1	28.9	2.5	2.0	30.3	2.4	5.0
Asia-Africa	100.0	4.3	1.7	8.7	30.9	1.8	2.7	38.3	3.3	8.3

Source: Jewish Agency for Palestine, *Statistical Handbook of Jewish Palestine, 1947*, pp. 66-67; Government of Palestine, *A Survey of Palestine*, Vol. 2, p. 732; Israel Central Bureau of Statistics, *Labour Force Survey, 1954*, Table 18, pp. 34-35, and Tables 22-25, pp. 42-51.

and direction, but of greater magnitude, are evident in the comparison of European and Oriental immigrants' distributions by occupations abroad. But the classification probably obscures certain differences between occupations of veteran settlers and of new immigrants, and especially between those of European and Oriental immigrants nominally in the same occupation categories. For the European veteran settlers, sales occupations abroad were likely to be in established retail or wholesale businesses whereas, for the Oriental immigrants, and to some extent for the new immigrants from Europe, sales occupations were likely to be peddling and hawking, petty trade, etc. For the European immigrants crafts, industrial, and building occupations were likely to be as wage and salary employees in some industrial or contracting establishment, while for the Oriental immigrants these occupations were likely to be as self-employed craftsmen and artisans.

Relative to the skills and experiences brought by immigrants both before and after 1948, the working force of the Jewish population of Palestine had much fewer sales occupations, somewhat fewer professional and technical occupations, many more agricultural occupations, more transport occupations, and evidently substantially more service and unskilled occupations. Again, although the comparison is tenuous, the labor force in post-independence Israel has had even fewer (relatively) sales occupations and even more agricultural, service, and unskilled occupations than the Jewish community in pre-independence Palestine.

The outstanding characteristics of the occupational patterns of the new immigrants in Israel in the first years is their relative exclusion from professional and technical, managerial, and clerical occupations and their concentration, relative to the veteran settlers, in agricultural, service, and unskilled occupations. This is the case for both European and Oriental new immigrants, but is much more pronounced in the case of the Oriental immigrants. More than half (50.6%) the employed Oriental new immigrants were in agricultural or unskilled occupations and only nine percent in professional, managerial, or clerical occupations (compared to 35.4% in these occupations among veteran settlers). A much larger percentage of the European new immigrants (21.9%) was absorbed in the professional, managerial, and clerical occupations, but fifteen percent were in unskilled occupations (compared to eight percent among the veteran settlers). Eleven percent were in agricultural occupations (compared to ten percent among the veteran settlers).

3

AFFAIRS OF STATE:
CHANGING SOCIAL BASES
OF ELECTORAL SUPPORT

I. GENERAL REMARKS

THE MOST REMARKABLE and also the most significant characteristic of Israel's political structure to date has been its
stability and continuity of national leadership in the face
of dramatic changes in population size and composition, two
wars with neighboring countries and constant external military and political pressures, ethnic and geo-cultural differences, religion vs. secularism cleavages, and sometimes-bitter
inter-party and intra-party political strife. In seventeen years
of independence Israel has had many government and coalition "crises" but only three Prime Ministers (D. Ben-Gurion,
M. Sharett, and L. Eshkol); only three Ministers of Defense
(Ben-Gurion and Eshkol have served in this capacity in
their governments; P. Lavon was Defense Minister in Sharett's
government); only three Ministers of Finance (E. Kaplan,
L. Eshkol, and P. Sapir); and only two Foreign Ministers
(M. Sharett and Mrs. G. Meir). While such a record may
suggest oligarchical or one-party control, in fact five full-
scale elections of new Parliaments (*Knesset*) have been
held. In each election candidates were listed and promoted
by no fewer than ten political parties, and no serious question
as to the honesty of national parliamentary elections has ever
been raised.

The political party drawing most votes, *Mapai*, with 34.7

percent of the vote in the last (1961) elections, has never drawn less than thirty-two percent nor more than thirty-nine percent of the vote. The religious parties together have consistently drawn about fifteen percent of the vote; the left-wing labor parties have consistently attracted between eleven and fifteen percent of the vote; and the right-of-center and right wing parties together have always polled between twenty and twenty-seven percent of the total votes in national parliamentary elections (Table 3.1). Many of the Israeli political, religious, or economic institutions which were pre-independence or early statehood loci of political power retain their strength and influence, e.g., the Rabbinate, the General Labor Federation (*Histadrut*), and the Zionist political parties; and, though some individual veteran political personalities have died, the survivors of pre-statehood politics have with few exceptions neither retired nor have they been dislodged from their positions.

But these elements of stability and continuity may operate to obscure certain major changes often held to have occurred since independence in the structure of political institutions in the Jewish population. The most important of these are:

1. the transfer of a wide range of social, economic, religious and political functions, responsibilities, initiative, and power from the hands of voluntary groups and organizations —usually parts of or connected with the pre-statehood organized Zionist enterprise—to the various ministries, bureaus, and departments of the Government of Israel. As noted in the first chapter, this transfer and some of its sociological implications were recognized and analyzed by Eisenstadt more than ten years ago in the very earliest years of Israel's independence, and his analysis was then and remains a cornerstone of social and political science in Israel.[1] The "de-voluntariza-

1. S. N. Eisenstadt, *The Absorption of Immigrants, op. cit.* See also S. N. Eisenstadt, "The Social Conditions of the Development of Voluntary Associations—A Case Study of Israel," *op. cit.*

TABLE 3.1.

RESULTS OF ELECTIONS TO THE *KNESSET* (PARLIAMENT), 1949-1961: PERCENT DISTRIBUTIONS BY PARTY LISTS

PARTY LIST	FIRST *Knesset* 25 JAN. 1949	SECOND *Knesset* 30 JULY 1951	THIRD *Knesset* 26 JULY 1955	FOURTH *Knesset* 3 DEC. 1959	FIFTH *Knesset* 15 AUG. 1961
Total	100.0	100.0	100.0	100.0	100.0
Mapai (Israel Labor (Party)	35.7	37.3	32.2	38.2	34.7
Mizrahi (Religious) & *Mizrahi* Workers	12.2 {	8.3	9.1	9.9	9.8
Agudat Israel (Orthodox Religious) & *Agudat Israel* Workers		3.6	4.7	4.7	5.6
Other Religious Lists	1.7	0.6	0.3	—	—
Herut (Freedom Party)	11.5	6.6	12.6	13.5	13.8
Mapam (United Workers Party)	14.7[a]	12.5[a]	7.3	7.2	7.5
Progressives	4.1	3.2	4.4	4.6 }	13.6[b]
General Zionists	5.2	16.2	10.2	6.2 }	
Communists	3.5	4.0	4.5	2.8	4.2
Ahdut Avodah (Unity of Labor)	a	a	8.2	6.0	6.6
Minorities and Other Lists	11.4	7.7	6.5	6.9	4.2

a. *Ahdut Avoda* List included in *Mapam*.

b. Liberal Party List.

Source: *Israel Central Bureau of Statistics, Statistical Abstract of Israel,* No. 13, Jerusalem, 1962, Part X, Table 1.

tion" of political structure and power in the Jewish community in Palestine and Israel has often since been cited as one of the most important facets of change in Israel.[2]

2. The "secularization," or departure from traditional

2. See Note 3 to Chapter 1. Also: A. Etzioni, "The Decline of Neo-Feudalism: The Case of Israel," paper presented at Annual Meeting of the American Political Science Association, St. Louis, Mo., September, 1961; and Y. Dror, "Public Policy Making in Israel" in Israel Institute of Public Administration, *Public Administration in Israel and Abroad, 1961* (Jerusalem, 1962).

religious observance and behavior, occurring especially inter-
generationally in the Oriental population.[3] Such a trend is of
great interest and importance both in its own terms and with
reference to popular support for the respective sides in the
secular-vs.-religious-state cleavage in Israel.

3. The change in the *bases* of political party differences and
of popular support for the respective political parties.[4] The
Zionist political parties in the *Yishuv* (the pre-independence
Jewish community of Palestine) were organized around and
distinguished by alternative *ideologies* concerning (*a*) the
nature and key institutions of the Jewish autonomous society
envisaged for the future and (*b*) the appropriate political
strategies for promoting Zionist interests in Palestine and for
rescue of Jews outside Palestine who were politically and
physically endangered prior to and during World War II.
But the political parties in independent Israel have been
increasingly viewed as distinguished by orientation to and
promotion of present or immediate future *interests* of the
various social, economic, residential, or ethnic subgroups, or
combinations of such subgroups, in the present population
of Israel from which electoral support is sought.

The problem in analysis of change in the political structure of Israel is not dissimilar to the more general problem
of analysis of change in social structure. Ideally it would be
desirable to be able:

1. to describe and characterize the political structure of
the *Yishuv*, the pre-independence Jewish community in
Palestine,

3. J. Matras, "Religious Observance and Family Formation in
Israel: Some Intergenerational Changes," *American Journal of Sociology,*
LXIX, No. 5 (March, 1964); S. D. Johnson, "Election Politics and So-
cial Change in Israel," *Middle East Journal,* Summer, 1962.

4. For background and description of Israeli political parties and
discussion on this point, see B. Akzin, "The Role of Parties in Israeli
Democracy," *Journal of Politics,* XVII, No. 4 (1955); E. E. Gutmann,
"Some Observations on Politics and Parties in Israel," *India Quarterly,*
XVII, No. 1 (1961); N. Safran, *The United States and Israel,* (Cam-
bridge, Mass., 1963) Chap. 8; and L. G. Seligman, *Leadership in a New
Nation* (New York, 1964).

2. to describe and characterize the political structure of Jewish communities abroad, and

3. to describe changes in the political structure of Israel since independence and show how these have been affected by (a) migration and transfer of political roles and institutions from Jewish communities abroad, and (b) growth and differentiation of the population of Israel, and (c) the emergence of an economically and politically independent, rather than dependent, society in Israel.

Generally for each society or social collectivity in each time period considered what is required is:

1. identification, description, and characterization of the different political roles, their interrelationships, and the stable relationships comprising the political institutions, including their manifest or explicitly-acknowledged purposes and aims,

2. analysis of the composition of the population by political roles and by attachment to political institutions, i.e., analysis of differential patterns of recruitment to political activity and support in the various population categories, and

3. analysis of the nature, structure, and distribution of the various types of power.

Unfortunately we are far from having the data on which to base such rigorous characterization or from having techniques enabling us to perform such an analysis.

The next section reviews 1. the argument concerning "de-voluntarization" of Israeli political structure and power, 2. some data bearing upon trends toward secularization or away from traditional religious observance and behavior, and 3. some data bearing upon the change from ideological to socio-economic and ethnic interest bases of political participation and support. The following section presents some preliminary results of an empirical study of social bases of electoral support for the respective political parties in Israel. The last section considers briefly some implications of the data presented and reviewed for changing political structure, participation, and support.

II. CHANGES IN THE POLITICAL WEIGHT OF VOLUNTARISM,
RELIGIOUS OBSERVANCE, AND IDEOLOGY.

The argument holding that the advent of independence
generated a wholesale transfer of political and bureaucratic
functions and authority from the hands of voluntary groups
and organizations for the State and at the same time created
a governing elite characterized by increasing social distance
from the population as a whole has received wide attention
and acceptance. Although systematic data bearing upon this
argument are not available, the transition from pre-independence political institutions operating in the Jewish community
of Palestine on a voluntary basis to the post-independence
State institutions with access to all the powers and sanctions
of legally constituted government may be reviewed briefly
by way of recapitulating the factual bases of this analysis.

Basically there were two Jewish autonomous political
institutions in Palestine: the Elected Assembly (*Asefat Niv-
harim*) and the Jewish Agency Executive, recognized (by the
British Mandatory Government and abroad) as representing
the interests of the Jewish community *resident* in Palestine
and the interests of World Jewry in Palestine. In addition
a large number and variety of voluntary Jewish organizations
operated in Palestine, the most important of which were the
Zionist political parties and the trade unions and General
Labor Federation (*Histadrut*).

The heart of the political structure of the Jewish community in Palestine as well as of the World Zionist Organization was a set of Zionist political movements and parties.
Ideological dissent and cleavage within the Zionist Organization concerning the nature and guiding principles of both
the Zionist movement and its operations and of governing the
Jewish community (which, it was agreed, was to be revived
and reestablished in Palestine) arose virtually with the very
beginnings of the Zionist movement.[5] The various groups and

5. A detailed analysis is given in B. Halpern, *op. cit.*

factions which organized Zionist ideological movements and parties divided on issues such as whether colonization and settlement should precede or follow world recognition of Jewish rights and interests in Palestine, religious or secular orientations, and socialism or collectivism vs. free enterprise; and each sought power and influence in the World Zionist Organization. Each of the Zionist parties typically operated on two levels: in Jewish communities throughout the world, and in the Jewish community in Palestine. A variety of activities was organized, including youth movements, cultural activities, and in some groups active promotion of immigration to Palestine. The parties sought supporters in the various Jewish communities and, through worldwide elections, the parties vied for representation in the World Zionist Congress, the deliberating body of the World Zionist Organization. In Palestine the parties sought to attract and organize recent immigrants and to hold the attachment of pre-immigration members; and they organized youth movements, settlement organizations, labor unions, social welfare and cultural activities, and very often economic enterprises.

In the early years of Jewish immigration to Palestine it was the Labor Zionist parties which were most successful in promoting and organizing immigration and in attracting and organizing recent Jewish immigrants in Palestine. Members of the labor parties organized the first trade unions and later the General Labor Federation (*Histadrut*). This latter organization undertook, in addition to promotion of labor interest in the usual ways, to found new cooperatives, industries, enterprises, and financial institutions as well as social welfare, medical, and cultural institutions. The General Labor Federation eventually became the largest single entrepreneur and employer in Palestine and hence a potent economic and political force. In the General Labor Federation periodic elections of leadership were held, and the Labor Zionist parties contested for positions of power and influence in this very important institution.

In Palestine the basic Zionist political party structure consisted of a network of local party branches, a national executive committee, and a national secretariat drawn, usually, from the executive committee. Associated with each party branch might be a network of youth organizations; and social, cultural, or economic activities such as adult education and Hebrew programs and courses, newspaper publishing, banks, housing developments, investment organizations, cooperative stores, life and medical insurance plans might be associated with either the local branches or with the national party machinery. In addition, if the party received sufficient support in balloting, it controlled a certain proportion of the positions and portfolios in the National Council (the executive arm of the Elected Assembly), Jewish Agency Executive, the Labor Federation, local governments, or in institutions where it sought power, and accordingly might have these additional areas of activity, initiative, and responsibility. Thus a party normally had a large number of both voluntary and paid positions to dispense to the faithful, and as the individual active member moved up the party ladder he could expect to assume more and more important positions within the party and in the institutions in which the party controlled positions. But the major source of party strength was in persons associated with party institutions at every level, identifying with party ideology, and expressing this identification in the various elections and balloting. The party sought always to attract individuals into its voluntary organizations and activities and to promote its ideology and solicit electoral support among them.

Thus, a most important characteristic of this entire network of activity is that it was almost entirely voluntary. For example, a family was not obliged to send its children to an Elected Assembly-supported school and, indeed, it was not obliged to send its children to any school at all. A person was not obliged to take part in military defense activities, and once involved, he was not obliged to remain. Jews immigrating to Palestine were not obliged to seek or accept either assistance or direction on the part of any of the Jewish institutions. Farm operators were free to market their produce inside or outside the cooperative marketing institutions; and individuals or groups were free to purchase and reclaim land without mediation of the Jewish National Fund or any other institution.

The nature of recruitment to political roles in the *Yishuv*, the pre-independence Jewish community in Palestine, remains problematic. The Zionist ideology was clearly democratic: all persons in the *Yishuv* had a right to participate in activities and to seek office; and it has been very widely assumed that participation in the Zionist political and economic enterprises and the distribution of power were essentially independent of other possible axes of social differentiation. But it is not really *known* whether or not in fact the different ethnic origin, period-of-immigration, religious or non-religious, occupation, or geographic groupings actually did or did not affect extent of participation in the political activities of the *Yishuv*. The fact that in Israel after achievement of independence there were widespread socially-based differences in the nature and extent of political participation suggests that this might well have been the case in the *Yishuv* as well. It is the *assumption* of perfect equality prior to statehood and independence which leads to the conclusion that the post-statehood inequality and differentiation in extent of participation reflects a *change* in the direction of inequality, development of strata, etc. This may indeed be the case, but the question is an empirical one and amenable to more satisfactory solution by research and investigation.

The political and military events leading to Great Britain's withdrawal from Palestine and to proclamation of an independent Jewish State, Israel, are well documented and need not be reviewed here.[6] However, it is worth recalling the manner in which the first provisional political institutions of

6. Recently published accounts include E. Rackman, *Israel's Emerging Constitution*, (New York, 1955); M. H. Bernstein, *The Politics of Israel* (Princeton, 1957), and O. Kraines, *Government and Politics in Israel*, (Boston, 1961).

independent Israel were organized. Essentially, the Palestine sectors of the Zionist political parties agreed to form a Provisional Government—to take over after the withdrawal of the Mandatory regime. This body was composed of the National Council (executive arm of the Elected Assembly) and the Palestine members of the Jewish Agency Executive, plus representatives of each of the Zionist and non-Zionist political parties not already represented by virtue of membership in one of the first two bodies.

In the early months of Statehood the various government ministries drew initially upon Jewish personnel in corresponding departments of the Mandatory Government and upon personnel of the corresponding departments of the National Council and the Jewish Agency Executive. Indeed, these departments of the National Council and the Jewish Agency were initially incorporated *en bloc* into the new Israel Government ministries. Additional personnel were recruited and added both to replace British and Arab incumbents of administrative posts and to fill new positions created in the attempt to handle the problems of the new nation and, especially, the problems of defense against the invading armies of neighboring states, and of reception of the tens of thousands of new immigrants.

New positions of power and authority were thus created, and the entire structure now had lawful authority and access to all the legal powers and sanctions of a sovereign state. The Zionist political parties, which previously had initiated, administered, and allocated resources and positions in a complex set of institutions in which participation and adherence on the part of Jewish residents of Palestine were *voluntary,* were now operating a government and a state, to which obedience and in which participation were mandatory on the part of all residents, Jew and non-Jew, Zionist and non-Zionist, old settler and new immigrant alike. In operating the government ministries, the parties had no alternative but to draw upon the personnel resources most familiar to them, those active in or closely associated with the respective Zionist parties and institutions in the pre-independence period. Accordingly, great concentrations of power passed into the hands of veteran party workers, especially of *Mapai,* but also of the other government coalition parties; and, whereas power and authority of these individuals were previously vested in voluntary acquiescence and participation on the part of the members of the various party institutions, now they were backed by the authority of government. Whereas previously the status of office was determined by voluntary relationships within a voluntary organization, now the status of office was fixed bureaucratically.

Not less important than the change in the nature of the relationships involved, changes in the nature of authority and spheres in which bureaucratic authority could now be exercised by incumbents of government roles occurred: the government, through its various economic powers, such as regulation of exchange of foreign currency, fixing of customs duties, and import licensing could support or subsidize an enterprise, group, individual, or institution, sometimes at the expense of other competing individuals or groups; or it could penalize groups, individuals, or enterprises in the same way. Similarly, the Government, usually through the institutions of the Immigration Department of the Jewish Agency, could direct settlement of new immigrants and manipulate and allocate resources and facilities among various veteran settlements and organizations. The authority over the military activities and service gave the government broad authority and powers over the lives and careers of individuals. In all the spheres, decisions were made and authority exercised in terms of the existing laws as interpreted and administered by the new incumbents who, in turn, were recruited and placed in their new roles by their party organizations.

In other words, the Government ministries, and the parties to which their administration was entrusted, were now charged with exercising authority and power in spheres bearing upon the daily economic and immediate material interest of all persons in the population and not just upon the ideological preferences of those voluntarily submitting to the authority in question. The Eisenstadt analysis of change in the social and political structure of the new State of Israel holds that the Zionist party activists and leadership, endowed with new powers, authority, and functions, and with their powers now bureaucratically based rather than dependent upon voluntary relationships, moved apart to a certain extent from the party and party-associated rank and file members and sympathizers. On the other hand, the voluntary organizations were deprived of many of their functions. Defense, education, reception of immigrants, colonization, and social welfare were now all government functions, and fund-raising was effected by taxation.

At the same time, the absolute number of persons and groups *not* involved in the pre-statehood voluntary associations of the Zionist parties grew very rapidly and spectacularly in the wake of the mass immigration to Israel. The new immigrants, for their part, were, according to Eisenstadt, inevitably oriented less to issues of state than to their own immediate personal and family needs: housing, employment and sustenance, medical care, and educational services for their children. Thus was generated a political situation in which the incumbent political party activists and leadership became increasingly an "establishment" removed both from the veteran settler population previously organized in close support of the autonomous political institutions of the *Yishuv* and from the new immigrant electorate never previously sympathetic to nor organized by the Zionist political movements and parties.[7]

Data bearing upon this question are not easily found, though two types of data would seem to be relevant. Analysis of the social, ethnic, and period-of-immigration origins and backgrounds of politically active persons—both prior to and immediately subsequent to achievement of independence—would offer some indication both of the population bases

7. See S. N. Eisenstadt, "The Social Conditions . . . of Voluntary Associations . . ." *op. cit.*, and other writings.

from which the support of the pre-statehood Zionist activities
was drawn and of the political bases of post-independence
Zionist party recruitment and support. For example, analysis
of party membership, of composition of membership "active"
at the various levels, etc., would indicate which population
groups, classified by place of residence, period of immigration, or by social, economic or occupational status, were
most and which were least frequently involved in political
action. Similarly, content analysis of party programs, of election campaign material, and of internal communications might
reveal the sources of party support and target populations
of the various party campaigns. Thus far such data have not
been developed and analyzed.

Some data bearing upon religious observance and changes
in its extent have recently become available. In an opinion
survey carried out by the Israel Institute of Applied Social
Research and reported by A. Antonovsky,[8] some thirty percent of Israeli respondents classified themselves "religious"
(observe all or most religious commandments), forty-six
percent reported that they "observe traditions to some extent,"
while twenty-four percent asserted themselves completely
secular ("not at all observant; completely secular"). In
response to the question, "Should the government see to it
that public life be conducted in accordance with Jewish
religious tradition?" some twenty-three percent replied, "Definitely, yes," and an additional twenty percent replied, "Probably yes." Negative replies were given by fifty-three percent
of the respondents, including thirty-seven percent replying
"definitely not" and sixteen percent replying "probably not"
with non-response accounting for the final four percent.

Responses to the two questions are cross-classified in Table
3.2. It would appear that not only do some seventy-nine percent of those reporting themselves personally religious favor
close ties between government and religion, but some twenty-
eight percent of those entirely secular or observant of only

8. A. Antonovsky, "Israeli Political-Social Attitudes," *Amot* (Hebrew), No. 6, 1963.

TABLE 3.2.

RESPONDENTS BY PERSONAL RELIGIOUS OBSERVANCE
AND BY OPINIONS CONCERNING TIES BETWEEN GOVERN-
MENT AND RELIGION (PERCENT DISTRIBUTION)[a]

	FAVOR GOVERNMENT PROMOTION OF RELIGIOUS TRADITION IN PUBLIC LIFE	REJECT GOVERNMENT PROMOTION OF RELIGIOUS TRADITION IN PUBLIC LIFE	TOTAL
Personally Religious	22%	6%	28%
Personally Secular or Partially Observant	19%	49%	68%
Total	41%	55%	96%

a. 4% Non-Response. See Text for source and relevant opinion-survey
questions.

some religious traditions also favor ties between religion
and government.

However, these data and the data of Chapter 2, concerning extent of religious observance viewed in relationship to
the data of Table 3.1 of this chapter showing percentage of the
vote polled by the religious parties, suggest strongly that
support of the religious political parties does not necessarily
follow from the fact of religious observance. The available
data suggest that the proportion of the population observing
religious traditions quite strictly is considerably greater than
the proportion of the vote received by the religious political
parties. Thus it would appear that the latter parties have
been less than spectacularly successful in convincing the
religious voters that their (the parties') demand that the
State of Israel embody the Torah and religious law and precepts in its constitution, legislation, and institutions deserves
support at the polls.

There are, moreover, many reasons to believe—and also, some data to support the belief—that a "secularization" trend of considerable proportions is occurring in Israel, and especially among the Oriental immigrants. Tables 3.3, 3.4, and 3.5 show the directions of integenerational change in extent of religious observance reported by the Jewish maternity cases interviewed in Israel in 1959/60.[9]

In the top panel of Table 3.3 it is seen that, though the maternity cases in Jerusalem are on the whole more religious than those in Tel Aviv-Jaffa, the mothers of both the Jerusalem and Tel Aviv-Jaffa groups are reported as more religious than the maternity cases. In the bottom panel of Table 3.3 it is seen that, of the Jerusalem maternity cases, fifty-nine percent were neither more nor less religious than their mothers, and a similar percentage, sixty-one percent, of the Tel-Aviv-Jaffa maternity cases reported themselves as religious as their mothers. But while forty percent of the Jerusalem maternity cases and thirty-seven percent of the Tel Aviv-Jaffa women reported themselves *less* religious than their mothers, almost none reported themselves more observant than their mothers. Thus the intergenerational change in extent of religious observance took place almost exclusively in a single direction—in the direction of diminishing religious observance.

In Table 3.4 this pattern is seen in more detail: the less observant the mothers, the more likely the daughters are to be as observant; the more observant the mothers, the more likely the daughters are to be less observant. Of the daughters of "observant" mothers, fifty-three percent in Jerusalem and forty-six percent in Tel Aviv-Jaffa reported themselves "observant" as well; but forty-seven percent in Jerusalem and more than half, fifty-four percent, in Tel Aviv-Jaffa reported themselves *less* religious than their mothers—the majority

9. Data are from the survey of maternity cases cited in Chapter 2 and have in part been previously reported in J. Matras, "Religious Observance . . . ," *loc. cit.*

TABLE 3.3.

JERUSALEM AND TEL AVIV MATERNITY CASES, 1959-60, BY PLACE OF BIRTH: CHANGE IN EXTENT OF OWN RELIGIOUS OBSERVANCE RELATIVE TO EXTENT OF MOTHERS' RELIGIOUS OBSERVANCE

RELIGIOUS OBSERVANCE CHARACTERISTICS (PERCENT DISTRIBUTIONS)	JERUSALEM				TEL AVIV			
	Total	Born in Israel	Born in America	Born in Asia, Africa	Total	Born in Israel	Born in America	Born in Asia, Africa
Number of Maternity Cases	582	198	94	290	180	54	39	87
RELIGIOUS OBSERVANCE OF MOTHER:								
Total	100.0	100.0	100.0	100.0	100.0	100.0	100.0	100.0
Observant	68.6	65.7	47.9	77.2	46.7	40.7	33.3	56.3
Partially-observant	22.2	23.7	26.6	20.0	31.1	31.5	28.2	32.2
Non-observant	9.1	10.6	25.5	2.8	22.2	27.8	38.5	11.5
OWN RELIGIOUS OBSERVANCE:								
Total	100.0	100.0	100.0	100.0	100.0	100.0	100.0	100.0
Observant	36.8	35.9	38.3	36.9	23.3	18.5	20.5	29.9
Partially-observant	41.9	36.8	24.5	51.0	36.7	33.3	41.0	34.5
Non-observant	21.3	27.3	37.2	12.1	40.0	48.2	38.5	35.6
MATERNITY CASES COMPARED TO MOTHERS:								
Total	100.0	100.0	100.0	100.0	100.0	100.0	100.0	100.0
As Religious as Mothers	59.4	59.6	76.6	53.8	60.6	59.2	84.6	50.6
More Religious than Mothers	0.9	2.0	1.1	0.0	2.8	1.9	2.6	3.4
Less Religious than Mothers	39.7	38.4	22.3	46.2	36.6	38.9	12.8	46.0

Source: R. Bachi and J. Matras, *Fertility and Contraception, Summary Tables of Surveys of Maternity Cases in Israel* (Jerusalem: Hebrew University Press, mimeographed, 1961).

TABLE 3.4.

MATERNITY CASES, JERUSALEM AND TEL AVIV, 1959-60, BY PLACE OF BIRTH, BY EXTENT OF MOTHERS' RELIGIOUS OBSERVANCE, AND BY EXTENT OF OWN RELIGIOUS OBSERVANCE (PERCENT DISTRIBUTION)

| Place of Birth and Extent of Mothers' Religious Observance | PLACE OF RESIDENCE AND EXTENT OF OWN RELIGIOUS OBSERVANCE | | | | | | | | | |
| | JERUSALEM | | | | | TEL AVIV | | | | |
	Nᵃ	Total	Observant	Partially Observant	Non-Observant	Nᵃ	Total	Observant	Partially Observant	Non-Observant
ALL PLACES OF BIRTH—TOTAL	582	100.0	36.8	41.9	21.3	180	100.0	23.3	36.7	40.0
Mothers Observant	399	100.0	52.9	39.6	7.5	84	100.0	46.4	38.1	15.5
Mothers Partially Observant	130	100.0	2.3	64.6	33.1	56	100.0	5.4	57.1	37.5
Mothers Non-Observant	53	100.0	0.0	3.8	96.2	40	100.0	0.0	5.0	95.0
BORN IN ISRAEL—TOTAL	198	100.0	35.9	36.8	27.3	54	100.0	18.5	33.3	48.2
Mothers Observant	130	100.0	52.3	32.3	15.4	22	100.0	45.5	40.9	13.6
Mothers Partially Observant	47	100.0	6.4	63.8	29.8	17	100.0	0.0	47.0	53.0
Mothers Non-Observant	21	100.0	0.0	4.8	95.2	15	100.0	0.0	6.7	93.3
BORN IN EUROPE-AMERICA—TOTAL	94	100.0	38.3	24.5	37.2	39	100.0	20.5	41.0	38.5
Mothers Observant	45	100.0	80.0	20.0	0.0	13	100.0	61.6	30.7	7.7
Mothers Partially Observant	25	100.0	0.0	52.0	48.0	11	100.0	0.0	100.0	0.0
Mothers Non-Observant	24	100.0	0.0	4.2	95.8	15	100.0	0.0	6.6	93.4
BORN IN ASIA-AFRICA—TOTAL	290	100.0	36.9	51.0	12.1	87	100.0	29.9	34.5	35.6
Mothers Observant	224	100.0	47.8	47.8	4.4	49	100.0	46.9	34.7	18.4
Mothers Partially Observant	58	100.0	0.0	70.7	29.3	28	100.0	10.7	46.4	42.9
Mothers Non-Observant	8	100.0	0.0	0.0	100.0	10	100.0	0.0	0.0	100.0

Source: Same as Table 3.3.

a. Maternity cases not reporting extent of mothers' religious observance allocated.

of the latter being "partially observant" (and *not* "non-observant") in both Jerusalem and Tel Aviv-Jaffa.

Among the daughters of "partially observant" mothers, the majority remained "partially observant;" but of those changing, almost all changed in the direction of "non-observance" rather than in the direction of more observance than their mothers. Of daughters of mothers who were "non-observant," almost all were themselves "non-observant"; none at all reported themselves "observant" and but one each in Jerusalem and in Tel Aviv-Jaffa reported themselves "partially observant."

Turning now to the comparison of intergenerational change in extent of religious observance in the different origin groups (Tables 3.3 and 3.4), pronounced differences between European and Oriental immigrant women are fairly evident. In both Jerusalem and Tel Aviv-Jaffa, European immigrant daughters of "observant" mothers were much more likely to report themselves also "observant" than were Oriental immigrant daughters of "observant" mothers. The Israeli-born daughters of "observant" mothers report change only slightly less frequently than do the Oriental immigrant women.

Some tentative hypotheses about duration-of-residence effects are possible on the basis of Tel Aviv data not presented here. In the case of European immigrants there is no basis for inferring great differences in extent of intergenerational change in religious observance between veteran settlers and new immigrants of European birth, the main conclusion for both European immigrant groups being that they are characterized by relative generation-wise stability. In the case of the Oriental veteran settler maternity cases, their distribution by extent of religious observance differs radically from that of their mothers, and in fact eighty-six percent of them reported change in the extent of religious observance relative to their mothers—all in the direction of diminished religious observance. By contrast, among Oriental new immigrant maternity cases the distribution by religious observance differed from that of their mothers, but not nearly so radically, and considerably less than half the women (41.0%) reported changes in extent of religious observance relative to their mothers. Moreover, not all the change was in the direction of diminished religious observance. Although less frequent change was reported by Oriental new immigrants than by Oriental veteran settler maternity cases, it is worth noting that the Oriental new immigrant maternity cases nevertheless reported more frequent intergenerational change in extent of religious observance than did either European new immigrants or European veteran settler maternity cases.

A number of additional comparisons are possible using the data for the Tel Aviv-Jaffa maternity cases. Table 3.5 indicates change in extent of religious observance relative to mothers for maternity cases born in Israel, in Europe, and in Asia and Africa, by number of school years completed. For maternity cases born in Israel or in Europe who are daughters of "observant" mothers, the likelihood of remaining "observant" is *higher* for those with post-primary education than for those with only primary education. More generally, the likelihood of changing relative to mothers' religious observance is evidently less for Israeli-born and European immigrant women with post-primary education than for such women with only primary education; and, although each individual index or measure depends upon a small number of cases, the same result appears for all measures. Thus half the women born in Israel who had completed only one to eight years of school reported some change in extent of religious observance relative to their mothers, but only one-third of those with nine or more school years completed reported themselves in religious observance categories different from those of their mothers. For women born in Europe twenty percent of those with one to eight years of school reported changes compared to twelve percent reporting changes among women completing nine or more years of school.

For Oriental immigrant maternity cases the relationship

TABLE 3.5.

JEWISH MATERNITY CASES, TEL AVIV, ISRAEL, 1959-60, BY PLACE OF BIRTH AND NUMBER OF SCHOOL YEARS COMPLETED: INDEXES OF CHANGE IN EXTENT OF OWN RELIGIOUS OBSERVANCE RELATIVE TO RELIGIOUS OBSERVANCES OF THEIR MOTHERS

PLACE OF BIRTH AND NUMBER OF SCHOOL YEARS COMPLETED	No.	PERCENT DISTRIBUTION				Proportion of Total Changing
		Total	As Religious	More Religious	Less Religious	
BORN IN ISRAEL—TOTAL	53	100.0	58.5	1.9	39.6	.415
1-8 years completed	26	100.0	50.0	0.0	50.0	.500
9+ " "	27	100.0	66.7	3.7	29.6	.333
BORN IN EUROPE-AMERICA—TOTAL	39	100.0	84.6	2.6	12.8	.154
1-8 years completed	15	100.0	80.0	0.0	20.0	.200
9+ " "	24	100.0	87.5	4.2	8.3	.125
BORN IN ASIA-AFRICA—TOTAL	87	100.0	52.9	3.4	43.7	.471
0 years completed	15	100.0	66.7	0.0	33.3	.333
1-8 " "	57	100.0	50.8	5.3	43.9	.492
9+ " "	13	100.0	46.7	0.0	53.3	.533
BORN IN ASIA-AFRICA—TOTAL	88	100.0	53.1	2.3	44.3	.466
Never Employed	29	100.0	69.0	0.0	31.0	.310
Employed prior to marriage	29	100.0	48.3	6.9	44.8	.517
Employed after marriage	30	100.0	43.3	0.0	56.7	.567

Source: Same as Table 3.3

between level of education and intergenerational change—
i.e., ordinarily diminishing—in religious observance category
is reversed and is a direct relationship. Of the maternity
cases whose mothers were reported "observant," one-third
(33.3%) of those with *no* education at all, fifty-eight percent
of those with at least some elementary education (1-8 years
of school) completed, and two-thirds (66.7%) of those with
at least some secondary education (9 or more years of school
completed) reported themselves in different—"partially-observant" or "non-observant"—religious observance categories
from those of their mothers. More generally, whereas one-
third of the women having no education reported change
(relative to their mothers) in religious observance category,
forty-nine percent of those completing one to eight years
of school, and fifty-three percent of those completing nine
or more years of school reported such change.

Almost all of the Tel Aviv maternity cases born in Israel
and in Europe had been employed at some time, and a large
majority had been employed after marriage. But of the women
born in Asia and Africa, only about a third had been employed after marriage, and another third had never been
employed at all. In Table 3.5 intergenerational change in
religious observance category is shown for the Oriental immigrant maternity cases in Tel Aviv-Jaffa by past labor force
attachment category.

Of the maternity cases whose mothers were "observant,"
and who themselves were never employed, more than two-
thirds reported themselves "observant" as well, and none
reported herself "non-observant." Of women with "observant"
mothers who *had* been employed at some time, only one
third remained "observant," half of the rest reporting themselves "partially observant" and the other half "non-observant."
Finally, a similar relationship is evident in the percentage
of each group reporting *any* change relative to mothers'
categories, the never-employed group reporting change least
frequently (31%), more than half (51%) of the employed-
before-marriage group reporting changes, and almost three-

fifths (57%) of the employed-after-marriage group reporting intergenerational changes.

Thus intergenerational change in extent of religious observance is very much more frequent among Oriental immigrants and among Israeli-born daughters than among the European immigrant women. Among European immigrants, there is little reason to conclude that there are duration-of-residence effects associated with inter-generational changes in religious observance; but for the Oriental immigrants there are evidently very marked duration-of-residence effects, the veteran settlers characterized by much more frequent intergenerational change in extent of religious observance than is the case for new immigrants. Among Israeli-born and European immigrants, post-primary education is evidently negatively associated with intergenerational change in the extent of religious observance. But among Oriental immigrants those who completed some post-primary education had the highest rates of intergenerational change, those attending no school at all had the lowest rates, and those attending only primary school had fairly high rates of change, but lower than those of the women with post-primary education. Finally, among Oriental women labor force attachments were positively associated with high frequencies of intergenerational change in extent of religious observance, and women who had never been employed outside their homes were characterized by lowest levels of such change. Thus although the European-born "observant" sectors appear to be relatively stable, it seems clear that—at least in Jerusalem and in Tel Aviv-Jaffa—the "observant" or religious sectors of the Israeli-born and Oriental immigrant population groups are experiencing large-scale "defection" to the "partially observant" and "non-observant" camps.

Especially the Oriental immigrant population (and the Israel-born population of Oriental origin as well) is evidently undergoing changes in extent of religious observance on a very broad scale, and there are many questions about the meaning of these changes. One possibility is that the religious observance attribute is simply another socio-economic attribute, negatively correlated with indexes of socioeconomic status, and change in which is closely related to changes in economic and educational opportunities, as reflected in data presented here. A possibility which does not necessarily contradict the "socio-economic attribute" formulation but is, nevertheless, of much more far-reaching implications is that the changes in religious observance represent more profound secularization trends or perhaps even the breakup and end of a—or of the several—traditional Oriental Jewish societies.

Data bearing upon the relationship between ideologies and political party support are available in the Israel Institute of Applied Social Research opinion survey reported by Antonovsky.[10] In pre-tests of the survey questionnaire, it was found that questions concerning voting intentions systematically elicited evasions on the part of a large minority of the respodents. Accordingly in the survey itself respondents were asked with which political trend they "identify," and four choices were offered: *Herut,* Center, Moderate Left, and Marxist Left. Those referring in their responses to specific parties were coded separately. Of the total twenty-four percent responded "Moderate Left" and another four percent gave *"Mapai"* as their response. The "Marxist Left" and *Mapam, Ahdut Avodah* and other Leftist responses accounted for an additional three percent of the responses; "Center" or "Liberals" were chosen by twenty-three percent, some five percent chose a religious party and eight percent chose *Herut.* Fully twenty-five percent gave answers indicating disinterest in politics and eight percent did not answer the question at all.

Referring to an earlier inquiry by Louis Guttman concerning unidimensional scalability of positions of Israeli parties on five major issues in Israeli political life,[11] Antonovsky

10. A. Antonovsky, *op. cit.,* and A. Antonovsky, "Political Ideologies of Israelis," *Amot* (Hebrew) No. 7, 1963.
11. L. Guttman, "Whither Israel's Political Parties," *Jewish Frontier,* Dec., 1961.

raises the question of unidimensional scalability of the attitudes of individual Israelis on the same issues, i.e., whether a set of political ideologies comprising attitudes on issues which can be ordered along a single dimension can be plotted for the Israeli electorate. On the basis of response to questions concerning East vs. West orientation, socialism vs. capitalism for Israel, attitude toward the *Histradrut* (General Labor Federation), and opinion concerning policy toward the Arab countries (activist vs. non-activist), Antonovsky concludes that, with certain exceptions, characteristic Israeli political ideologies *do* form a unidimensional scale as follows:

Scale Type

1. Pro-USSR economic system,
   pro-socialism in Israel,
   pro-*Histadrut*, and
   anti-activist
   (2%)

2. Pro-US economic system,
   pro-socialism in Israel,
   pro-*Histadrut*, and
   anti-activist
   (8%)

3. Pro-US economic system,
   not strongly pro-socialism in Israel,
   pro-*Histadrut*, and
   anti-activist
   (22%)

4. Pro-US economic system,
   not strongly pro-socialism in Israel,
   anti-*Histadrut*, and
   anti-activist
   (23%)

5. Pro-US economic system,
   not strongly pro-socialism in Israel,
   anti-*Histadrut*, and
   pro-activist
   (19%)

In addition, there is a deviant type,

6. Pro-US economic system,

not strongly pro-socialism in Israel,
pro-activist, and
pro-*Histadrut*.
(10%)

which, Antonovsky suggests, may correspond to what may
be called the "right wing of *Mapai*." Finally there is a quite
considerable group of respondents classified as "non-ideological" (16%) comprising persons who did not answer enough
of the questions to permit their inclusion in the analysis.
Antonovsky continues to analyze the political trend identification, and objective socio-economic characteristics of those
characterized by the respective ideological types. Quite a
number of questions are raised by the unique data and analysis presented, but what is of particular interest in the present
context is the analysis of the composition of those identifying
with the various political trends by ideological types.[12]

The relevant data are reproduced in Table 3.6. The latter
suggest that *all* the political parties and trends derive *some*
support from all but one of the ideological types. The
Marxist Left trend is virtually the only one deriving support
from Type 1, the most extreme Left ideological type, and
even this trend receives most of its support from other ideological types.

Support for or identification with the Moderate Left—
including, especially, *Mapai*—is drawn from the greatest range
of ideological types, while identification with the Center
tends to be most concentrated. All the political trends except the Center receive a not inconsiderable proportion of
their support from persons in the "non-ideological" category, a category which doubtless does include many who
actually do not hold clearly conceived or formulated ideologies.

Thus not only must each of the political parties and
trends compete for support among persons of different ideological learnings, but the parties must also compete for the
support of persons not holding any clear-cut ideology and

12. A. Antonovsky, "Political Ideologies . . ." *op. cit.*, Table 4.

TABLE 3.6.

SOURCES OF SUPPORT FOR POLITICAL PARTIES AND TRENDS, BY IDEOLOGICAL TYPES (PERCENT DISTRIBUTIONS)*

| POLITICAL PARTIES AND TRENDS | NO. | TOTAL | IDEOLOGICAL TYPES | | | | | | NON-IDEO-LOGICAL |
			1	2	3	4	5	6	
Marxist Left[a]	29	100	17	17	28	10	7	10	11
Moderate Left[b]	337	100	2	9	26	25	17	12	9
Center[c]	266	100	0	4	27	34	24	7	4
National Religious Party	52	100	2	10	11	27	27	8	15
Herut	98	100	1	7	21	15	26	23	7
Not Interested in Politics	289	100	3	7	19	17	15	9	30
Others	99	100	1	11	12	17	10	6	43
Total	1,170	100	2	8	22	23	19	10	16

* See Text for source and specification of Ideological Types
a. Includes those responding *"Mapam,* workers, socialist," etc.
b. Includes those responding *"Mapai"*
c. Includes those responding "Liberals"

presumably, for the support of a share of the twenty-five percent not interested in politics. If these data correctly reflect the relationship between individual ideological leanings and support for political trends and parties, and if this interpretation is correct, it follows that the respective parties must make themselves congenial to ideologically diverse and heterogeneous ideas, elements, and support; and it seems reasonable to suppose that such flexibility necessarily implies relatively less weight and importance of ideology itself in Israeli parties.

That this is the impression of many Israeli politicians themselves is suggested by data collected by L. G. Seligman and his students.[13] Of ninety Members of *Knesset* in-

13. L. G. Seligman, *op. cit.,* Chap. 3.

terviewed, fifty (or 56%) agreed that newer sources of political leadership are less ideological than were the old-timers. In a study of unsuccessful candidates from *Mapai* and *Herut* for election to the *Knesset*, M. Telem found that only a minority of those interviewed (33% among the 57 *Mapai* candidates, and 48% among the 71 *Herut* candidates) felt that ideological motives exclusively should guide the electorate. The majority felt that voting should be based upon both ideological and pragmatic considerations.[14]

Seligman has distinguished three types among Israeli parties:

1. Sectarian, characterized by strong ideological coherence and discipline, and including the Religious *Poale Agudat Israel* and *Agudat Israel* parties and the anti-clerical *Ahdut Avodah*.
2. Populist, characterized by weak party structure and diffuseness of their broad nationalistic ideology, including *Herut*, the General Zionists, and the Communist party.
3. Pluralists, those parties which integrate diverse groups, including *Mapam*, Progressives (now combined with General Zionists in the Liberal Party), *Mapai*, and the National Religious Party.

With respect to the weight of ideology in Israeli politics, Seligman summarized his data for the three types of parties as follows:

In general, on questions involving the viability of traditional values, the populists perceive ideological decline, whereas the sectarians reaffirm the vitality of ideologies. The pluralists, who are rooted in a strong ideological past and yet are very receptive to new developments, reflect a dualism that points in both directions.[15]

14. M. Telem, "Politicians in Israel." Unpublished M.A. thesis (in Hebrew). Department of Political Science, The Hebrew University, pp. 108-113.
15. L. G. Seligman, *op. cit.*, p. 84.

III. SOCIAL BASES OF POLITICAL PARTY SUPPORT IN THE 1961
PARLIAMENTARY ELECTIONS: SOME PRELIMINARY DATA.[16]

Beginnings of an empirically-grounded analysis of social
bases of electoral support for the various parties in Israel
are possible utilizing 1961 election data in conjunction with
returns of the 1961 Israel Census of Population and Housing.
Results of elections to the *Knesset* are published for the
entire country by districts, by cities and other places of residence, by sub-areas within cities, and by election districts or
precincts within the cities and smaller cities. Of course it has
not been possible to know demographic or socio-economic
characteristics of persons voting for the respective parties.
But for 1961, the year of Israel's recent census, demographic
and socio-economic data are available in considerable detail
for the populations of individual cities, settlements, and a
variety of combinations of sub-areas.[17] Use of the census
data in conjunction with the election data permit an empirical analysis of ethnic origin and socio-economic bases of
support in the 1961 elections for the various parties in Israel
by means of techniques commonly known as "ecological
correlation" or "ecological regression."[18]

16. Data presented in this section are first findings from a study
of social bases of support for political parties in Israel in collaboration
with E. E. Gutmann. Findings and conclusions of the study will be reported separately and in detail. Prof. Gutmann has kindly read an
earlier draft of this chapter and offered very helpful comments and
suggestions; but responsibility for the materials presented and their interpretation here rests entirely with the author.
17. CBS, *Results of Elections to the Fifth Knesset* (Jerusalem,
1964). See also Israel Central Bureau of Statistics publications of results of the Census of Population and Housing, 1961, and especially
the series subtitled, *Settlements of Israel*.
18. The technical literature includes: W. S. Robinson, "Ecological
Correlations and the Behavior of Individuals," *American Sociological
Review*, XV (1950); L. A. Goodman, "Ecological Regression and Behavior of Individuals," *American Sociological Review*, XVIII (1953);
O. D. Duncan and B. Davis, "An Alternative to Ecological Correlation," *American Sociological Review*, (XVIII 1953); and L. A. Good-

Basically this approach involves using separate (not cross-classified) data on proportions voting for the various parties and on proportions belonging to the various ethnic or socio-economic categories in all of the several geographic units to measure the correlation between ethnic- or socio-economic category composition and party composition of the vote. It is important to distinguish between "ecological correlations" and "individual correlations": a high positive "ecological correlation" between country of birth i and political party j indicates that cities characterized by relatively high proportions (relative to the mean proportion) born in country i tend also to be characterized by relatively high proportions (relative to the mean proportion) voting for party j; that cities characterized by relatively low proportions born in country i tend also to be characterized by relatively low proportions voting for party j—and *not necessarily* that persons born in country i tend to vote for party j. Similarly a high negative "ecological correlation" between country of birth i and party j must be viewed as indicating that cities with relatively high proportions born in country i tend to show relatively low proportions voting for party j, and conversely and *not necessarily* that persons born in country i tend to avoid voting for party j.

The coefficients of "ecological correlation" between percentages of foreign-born population born in each of the major countries or areas of birth and percentages of valid (1961 elections) votes for each of the four largest political parties or trends are given in Table 3.7 for the seventeen cities with Jewish populations totaling 20,000 or more in

man, "Some Alternatives to Ecological Correlation," *American Journal of Sociology,* LXIV (1959). See also O. D. Duncan, "Human Ecology and Population Studies" in P. M. Hauser and O. D. Duncan, ed., *The Study of Population: An Inventory and Appraisal,* (Chicago: University of Chicago Press, 1959); and O. D. Duncan, R. Cuzzort, and B. Duncan, *Statistical Geography: Problems in Analyzing Areal Data* (Glencoe, Ill.: The Free Press, 1960). Examples of applications of this approach are cited in the Robinson article. For a more recent application, see D. Mac-Rae, Jr., "Occupations and the Congressional Vote, 1940-1950," *American Sociological Review,* XX (1955).

TABLE 3.7.

ECOLOGICAL CORRELATIONS BETWEEN COUNTRY OF BIRTH, COMPOSITION AND 1961 NATIONAL PARLIAMENTARY ELECTIONS VOTE FOR MAJOR PARTIES

		COUNTRIES OF BIRTH			
PARTIES	Iraq	Morocco, Algeria, Tunisia	Rumania	Poland, USSR	Germany, Austria
Mapai	−.41	.25	.20	.20	−.14
Religious Parties	.43	.04	.03	−.38	−.16
Herut	.40	.37	−.73	−.47	−.36
Liberal Party	−.36	−.65	.24	.82	.82

1961.[19] The seventeen cities represented included sixty-five percent of the total Jewish population, and sixty-four percent of the foreign-born Jewish population of Israel in May 1961. The country- or area-of-birth groups represented included sixty-seven percent of the total foreign-born Jewish population of Israel in 1961, and the four political parties or groups received together seventy-eight percent of the total vote in the 1961 national elections.

In Table 3.7 it is seen that cities with high proportions born in Iraq tend to show support for *Herut,* the right-wing nationalist-activist party, on the one hand and for the Religious parties, on the other hand; and *Mapai,* the left-of-center labor party, and the right-of-center Liberal party make relatively poor showings in such cities. Cities with relatively large numbers of North African-born immigrants show support for *Mapai,* while the Liberal party tends to fare relatively poorly in such cities. Cities with large percentages born in Rumania show some support for the Liberal party and for *Mapai,* but especially such cities show the *Herut* party doing quite poorly. The Liberal party receives quite strong

19. The cities are Jerusalem, Tel Aviv-Jaffa, Haifa, Ashkelon, Be'ersheba, B'nai Berak, Bat Yam, Givatayim, Hadera, Holon, Tiberias, Netanya, Petah Tikva, Rishon Lezion, Rehovot, Ramla, and Ramat Gan.

support in cities with high percentages born in Poland and
the USSR and in cities with high percentages born in Germany and Austria; while *Herut* tends to fare quite poorly in
such cities.

Considered from the point of view of the parties: *Mapai*
is characterized by positive ecological correlations with Rumania and with North Africa, negative ecological correlations
with Germany and Austria and, especially, with Iraq. The
Religious parties are characterized by a positive ecological
correlation with Iraq, by negative ecological correlations
with Germany and Austria and, especially, with Poland and
the USSR. *Herut* is seen to be characterized by substantial
positive ecological correlations with Iraq and with North
Africa, by substantial negative ecological correlations with
Germany and Austria, with Poland and the USSR, and,
especially, with Rumania. Finally the Liberal party is characterized by quite high positive ecological correlations with
Germany and Austria and with Poland and the USSR, by
a less spectacular positive ecological correlation with Rumania, by a moderate negative ecological correlation with
Iraq, and by a more substantial negative ecological correlation with North Africa.

The possibility of making certain limited types of inferences concerning individual behavior on the basis of
"ecological regressions" has been pointed out by L. A. Goodman;[20] and if the restrictions are born in mind, some inferences may be made concerning support for the various
political parties by individuals in the several country-of-birth
categories as well as country-of-birth composition of the
total vote for each of the parties in the 1961 elections. If
persons "born in country i" and those "not born in country
i" are cross-classified by "voting for party j" or "not voting
for party j" as follows:

20. L. A. Goodman, "Some Alternatives to Ecological Regression,"
op. cit.

PLACE OF BIRTH BY PARTY VOTE IN 1961 ELECTIONS

	Born in Country i	Not Born in Country i	Total—All Places of Birth
Voting for Party j	A	B	A + B
Not Voting for Party j	C	D	C + D
Total—Voting for All Parties	A + C	B + D	A + B + C + D

and if the marginal totals or proportions are known for a number of geographical areas, it is possible to estimate the proportions:

$$\frac{A}{A+B} = \text{proportion voting for party } j \text{ among all persons born in country } i$$

and

$$\frac{A}{A+C} = \text{proportion born in country } i \text{ among all persons voting for party } j.$$

provided that it is reasonable to suppose that these proportions, $A/A + C$ and $A/A + B$, are approximately constant over the geographic areas considered.

It is clear that the country-of-birth-party-vote cross-classification in the present case is *not* a double-dichotomous cross-classification; and there is no basis for assuming that the proportions of the form $A/A + C$ and $A/A + B$, are necessarily constant, or even very close to one another, in the various cities. Nevertheless it is of interest to compare their relative magnitudes as first-approximations or very gross indicators of political leanings in the various area-of-birth population groups and of ethnic sources of support for the various parties.

The estimated proportions of each area-of-birth group voting for each of the respective parties (proportions of the form $A/A + C$, as above) are shown in the top panel of Table 3.8; while estimated proportions of each party's total vote derived from among each of the country-of-birth groups (proportions of the form $A/A + B$, as above) are shown in the bottom panel of the same table. The data are for the seventeen Israeli cities with 20,000 or more Jewish population in 1961. It suffices to note that there are both *negative* numbers and numbers *greater than unity* among the estimated proportions (which, of course, should be positive numbers between zero and unity) in order to confirm the inapplicability of the assumptions cited above. However, the *comparison* of the estimates is of some interest in the present context.

The estimates of the top panel of Table 3.8 suggest that immigrants born in Iraq tend to split their votes between the Religious parties and *Herut,* while those born in Morocco, Algeria, and Tunisia tend to split their votes among *Mapai, Herut,* and the Religious parties. Among those born in Iraq the Religious parties appear to receive almost twice the support as does *Herut,* while among those born in North Africa *Mapai* appears to receive as much support as do the Religious parties and *Herut* combined. Both the born-in-Rumania and the born-in-Poland or the USSR groups show support for both *Mapai* and the Liberal Party, the Rumanian-born immigrants favoring *Mapai* and the Poland-USSR-born immigrants favoring the Liberal party. In addition the Rumanian immigrant group indicates not inconsiderable support for the Religious parties. Finally, the immigrants born in Germany and Austria would appear, from these estimates, to concentrate their voting support quite heavily in favor of the Liberal party.

The estimates of the bottom panel of Table 3.8 suggest that support for *Mapai* and for the Religious parties cuts

TABLE 3.8.

ESTIMATED PROPORTIONS VOTING FOR THE RESPECTIVE PARTIES IN EACH COUNTRY OF BIRTH CATEGORY AND ESTIMATED PROPORTIONS FROM AMONG THE RESPECTIVE COUNTRY OF BIRTH CATEGORIES IN THE TOTAL VOTE FOR EACH PARTY, 1961

ESTIMATED PROPORTIONS VOTING FOR THE RESPECTIVE PARTIES IN EACH COUNTRY OF BIRTH CATEGORY

		COUNTRIES OF BIRTH			
PARTIES	Iraq	Morocco, Algeria, Tunisia	Rumania	Poland, USSR	Germany, Austria
Mapai	.08	.47	.58	.36	−.06
Religious Parties	.68	.20	.24	−.06	−.62
Herut	.36	.27	−.38	.05	−.55
Liberal Party	−.11	−.14	.30	.43	2.89
All Parties[a]	(1.00)	(1.00)	(1.00)	(1.00)	(1.00)

ESTIMATED PROPORTIONS FROM AMONG THE RESPECTIVE COUNTRY OF BIRTH CATEGORIES IN THE TOTAL VOTE FOR EACH PARTY

		COUNTRIES OF BIRTH				
PARTIES:	Iraq	Morocco, Algeria, Tunisia	Rumania	Poland, USSR	Germany, Austria	All Countries[a]
Mapai	−.21	.44	.23	.29	.01	(1.00)
Religious Parties	.39	.15	.15	−.10	.01	(1.00)
Herut	.75	1.03	−.66	−.90	−.11	(1.00)
Liberal Party	−.27	−1.03	.30	2.04	.30	(1.00)

a. Indicates direction of summation only; not equal to sum to estimated proportions.

119

across the European immigrant-Oriental immigrant division; while support for *Herut* appears to be concentrated among Oriental immigrants and support for the Liberal party appears to be concentrated among European immigrants. *Mapai* appears to receive very little support from among those born in Germany and Austria, no support (negative estimate) from among those born in Iraq, but substantial support among those born in North Africa, in Rumania, and in Poland and the USSR. The Religious parties receive a substantial proportion of their support from among immigrants born in Iraq and some support among those born in North Africa and in Rumania respectively. Support for *Herut* is derived both from immigrants born in Iraq and from those from North Africa. The largest component of support for the Liberal party seen in these data is that provided by immigrants from Poland and the USSR, though substantial support is provided by the other two European immigrant groups shown.

Computation of coefficients of "ecological correlation" between proportions having specified socio-economic characteristics and proportions voting for the several parties can be carried out in the same manner as were computed the coefficients relating countries of birth and the vote; and their interpretation is similarly of the form: high "ecological correlation" coefficients between characteristic i and party j imply that cities with relatively high proportions of the population having socio-economic characteristic i tend to have relatively high proportions voting for party j, and conversely. Computations of coefficients of "ecological correlation" between party vote and composition by economic branch of the employed labor force and by years-of-school completed by the adult (aged $25 +$) population were carried out for two groups of cities of 5,000 or more Jewish inhabitants in 1961, as follows:

1. European Veteran Settler" towns: including nine
   towns[21] at least one-half of whose populations in

21. Tel Aviv-Jaffa, Haifa, B'nei Berak, Givatayim, Pardess Hana, Kiryat Tivon, Kiryat Motzkin, Kiryat Bialik, Ramat Gan.

1961 comprised persons born in Israel or immigrating prior to 1948, and at least two-thirds of whose foreign-born populations were born in Europe, North or South America, or Oceania.

2. "Oriental New Immigrant" towns: including eight towns[22] at least one-half of whose populations in 1961 comprised persons immigrating to Israel in 1948 or later, and at least two thirds of whose foreign-born populations were born in Asia, Africa, or the Middle-East.

A correspondingly defined "Oriental Veteran Settler" town category would include only a single town, Tiberias, while a similar "European New Immigrant" town category would include only three towns: Nahariya, Nesher, and Bat Yam.

In general, to the extent that political ideologies and political party support tend to be congruent with socio-economic status or characteristics, fairly high ecological correlations would be expected between given socio-economic categories and the vote for the parties with whose ideologies they are expected to identify, e.g., between "workers" and "left-wing" parties, or between "business and professional" groups and "center" or "right-of-center" parties. Conversely, to the extent that party appeal cuts across social or economic status divisions, no such pattern of correlations between socio-economic groups and the vote for the corresponding political parties would be evident. Unfortunately, the present data do not have reference to homogeneous social or economic status categories, so that their validity for inferring congruence between political party support and socio-economic characteristics or status is, at best, indirect and limited.[23] Only the "zero-school-years completed" category may be presumed

22. Or Yehuda, Ashkelon, Beth Shan, Beth Shemesh, Dimona, Yavne, Kiryat Shmonah, Rosh Ha'ayin.

23. Census data on occupational composition of the employed for individual cities were not yet available. A corresponding analysis using occupational categories instead of economic branch categories is planned as data become available.

fairly homogeneous with respect to socio-economic status.

The coefficients of "ecological correlation" between economic branch composition and support for the various political parties and between educational achievement composition and political party support are shown in Table 3.9 for the nine "European Veteran Settler" towns (top panel) and for the eight "Oriental New Immigrant" towns (bottom panel). Both in order to reduce the total number of comparisons and to try to focus upon the least doubtful of the relationships indicated by these computations, the data are recapitulated in Table 3.10 using the following procedure:

1. Coefficients of "ecological correlations" with absolute values less than .25 are ignored altogether or, rather, reproduced in Table 3.10 as 0.

2. Coefficients of "ecological correlation" with absolute values .25 or greater but less than .40 are rendered in Table 3.10 as + or as − according as they are positive or negative in Table 3.9; i.e., account is taken of their signs but not of their magnitudes.

3. Coefficients of "ecological correlation" with absolute values .40 or greater are reproduced in Table 3.10 as they appear originally in Table 3.9.

4. In addition to the coefficients of "ecological correlation," the mean percentages of the 1961 vote for each of the parties, and the mean percentages in each of the economic branch and educational achievement categories are shown for the "European Veteran Settler" towns and for the "Oriental New Immigrant" towns respectively.

In both the "European Veteran Settler" and the "Oriental New Immigrant" towns there are substantial positive ecological correlations between proportion employed in commerce and services and the vote for *Mapai;* and there are substantial negative ecological correlations between the proportion employed in commerce and services and the vote for the Religious parties. In both types of communities the vote for

TABLE 3.9.

"EUROPEAN VETERAN SETTLER" AND "ORIENTAL NEW IMMIGRANT" CITIES AND TOWNS: ECOLOGICAL CORRELATIONS BETWEEN COMPOSITION BY ECONOMIC BRANCH AND PARTY VOTE, AND BETWEEN COMPOSITION BY EDUCATIONAL ACHIEVEMENT AND PARTY VOTE, 1961

	ECONOMIC BRANCHES			YEARS OF SCHOOL COMPLETED		
	Agriculture	Manufacturing, Construction	Commerce, Services	0 Years	1-8 Years	9+ Years
"EUROPEAN VETERAN SETTLER" TOWNS:						
Mapai	.03	−.68	.40	−.51	−.65	.57
Religious Parties	.28	.59	−.54	.57	.74	−.75
Herut	−.31	.26	.29	.30	.19	−.11
Liberal Party	−.34	−.28	.26	−.55	−.73	.68
Achdut Avoda	.00	−.56	.56	−.46	−.53	.77
Mapam	−.24	−.14	.02	−.72	−.46	.58
Not Voting	−.32	−.57	.54	.28	.32	−.11
"ORIENTAL NEW IMMIGRANT" TOWNS:						
Mapai	−.07	.15	.82	−.83	.79	−.74
Religious Parties	.28	−.38	−.45	.81	−.90	−.56
Herut	−.51	.50	−.03	−.02	.16	−.20
Liberal Party	.13	−.26	−.14	.06	−.12	.28
Ahdut Avodah	.00	.16	−.12	.47	.58	.09
Mapam	.32	−.08	.14	.56	.34	.58
Not voting	−.51	.65	−.29	.26	.34	.09

123

TABLE 3.10.

"EUROPEAN VETERAN SETTLER" AND "ORIENTAL NEW IMMIGRANT" CITIES AND TOWNS: COMPOSITION OF THE EMPLOYED POPULATION BY ECONOMIC BRANCH; COMPOSITION OF THE ADULT (AGED 25+) POPULATION BY NUMBER OF SCHOOL YEARS COMPLETED; COMPOSITION OF THE 1961 PARLIAMENTARY ELECTIONS VOTE BY PARTIES; AND ECOLOGICAL CORRELATIONS BETWEEN COMPOSITIONAL CHARACTERISTICS AND PARTY VOTE[a]

	COMPOSITION OF 1961 VOTE (PERCENT)[b]	ECONOMIC BRANCHES			SCHOOL YEARS COMPLETED		
		Agri-culture	Manufac-turing con-struction	Commerce, Services	0 Years	1-8 Years	9+ Years
"EUROPEAN VETERAN SETTLER" TOWNS:							
Composition by Economic Branch and Educational Achievement (Percent)[b]		3.00	38.11	40.56	6.56	40.56	50.78
ECOLOGICAL CORRELATIONS:							
Mapai	38.00	0	−.68	+.40	−.51	−.65	+.57
Religious Parties	15.33	+	+.59	−.54	+.57	+.74	−.75
Herut	11.33	−	+	+	+	0	0
Liberal Party	19.22	0	−.56	+.56	−.55	−.73	+.68
Ahdut Avodah	6.22	0	0	0	−.46	−.53	+.77
Mapam	7.00	0	−.57	+.54	−.72	−.46	+.58
Not Voting	16.00	−			+	+	0

"ORIENTAL NEW IMMIGRANT" TOWNS:

	(Percent)	Composition by Economic Branch and Educational Achievement (Percent)b					
		15.62	44.75	25.25	36.38	44.75	25.25
Mapai	36.00						
Religious Parties	28.62						
Herut	17.12						
Liberal Party	3.75						
Ahdut Avodah	6.38						
Mapam	5.88						
Not Voting	20.88						
ECOLOGICAL CORRELATIONS:							
Mapai		0	0	+.82	—	+.79	+.74
Religious Parties		+	—	-.45	+.81	-.90	-.56
Herut		-.51	+.50	0	0	0	0
Liberal Party		0	—	0	0	0	+0
Ahdut Avodah		0	0	0	+.47	+.58	0
Mapam		+	0	0	+.56	+	+.58
Not Voting		-.51	+.65	—	+	+	0

a. See text for list of cities, source of data.

b. Excludes "Unknown," and percentages do not add to 100.0%

125

Herut is correlated positively with the proportion employed in manufacturing and construction and negatively with the proportion employed in agriculture; and the Liberal party vote is correlated negatively with the proportion employed in manufacturing and construction. In both groups of communities the proportion employed in agriculture is correlated positively with the vote for the Religious parties and negatively with failure to vote at all.

In both types of communities the proportion with no formal education (0 school years completed) is characterized by high positive ecological correlation with the vote for the Religious parties and high negative ecological correlation with the vote for *Mapai*. Conversely, the proportion with post-primary education (9 + school years completed) is positively correlated with the vote for *Mapai*, and negatively correlated with the vote for the Religious parties, in both "European Veteran Settler" and in "Oriental New Immigrant" towns. In both types of communities the vote for the right-of-center Liberal party is positively correlated with the proportion having post-primary education; but so, also, is the vote for the left-wing *Mapam* correlated positively with the proportion having post-primary education.

The major differences between the "European Veteran Settler" communities and the "Oriental New Immigrant" communities revolve around the vote for the left-wing *Mapam* and *Ahdut Avodah* parties and around non-voting. In the European Veteran Settler communities there are negative coefficients of ecological correlation between low educational achievement and the vote for *Mapam* and *Ahdut Avodah,* and positive correlations between high (post-primary) educational achievement and the vote for these two left-wing parties. But in the Oriental New Immigrant communities there are positive coefficients of ecological correlation between low educational achievement and the vote for *Mapam* and *Ahdut Avodah*. In the European Veteran Settler communities employment in manufacturing and construction is negatively correlated with failure to vote, while employment in commerce and in government and business services is positively correlated with failure to vote. But in the Oriental New Immigrant communities failure to vote is positively correlated with employment in manufacturing and construction and negatively correlated with employment in commerce and services.

The question of correspondences between political ideologies and party support and social or economic characteristics or status seems best examined in the data at hand from the point of view of which socio-economic groups or categories "embrace" or "reject" which political parties. Looking first in Table 3.10 at the Economic Branch categories represented in the first three columns, it seems clear that clear-cut "embracing" or "rejection" of political parties in such heterogeneous categories is quite infrequent. However, looking at the Educational Achievement category columns of Table 3.10, a pattern of "embracing" and "rejection" of parties does emerge, if only in rude outlines. In the European Veteran Settler towns the low-education categories (*both* 0 years and 1-8 years are "low" in these towns) "reject" *Mapai*, "reject" the Liberal Party, and "reject" the left-wing parties (*Mapam* and *Ahdut Avodah*) and "embrace" the Religious parties, while the high-education categories (9 + years) do exactly the reverse. In the Oriental New Immigrant towns the low-education categories (0 years of school) also "reject" *Mapai* and "embrace" the Religious parties. But the low-education category is also attracted quite strongly to the two left-wing labor parties in these communities. The more educated category (1-8 years *and* 9 + years, in the Oriental Communities) "embrace" *Mapai* and "reject" the Religious parties, and tend also to "embrace" the left-wing parties, but *not* the liberal party.

The absence of coefficients of ecological correlation of any substantial magnitude between the educational achievement categories and the vote for *Herut* in both types of communities suggests that *Herut* is equally popular (in the Oriental New Immigrant communities) or equally unpopular (in the European Veteran Settler communities) among the separate educational achievement categories. The absence of substantial coefficients of ecological correlation between the vote for the Liberal party and the educational achievement categories among the Oriental New Immigrant towns suggests, similarly, that in these communities the Liberal party is about equally unpopular in all three of the different educational achievement subgroups.

IV. SOME ISSUES AND RESEARCH PROBLEMS

Two kinds of issues are raised by the data reviewed and presented in the preceding sections of this chapter. The first problem concerns the description itself of the relationship between the political parties and the various socio-economic population categories—its validity, reliability and completeness—and its bearing upon the relationships between the political structure and other facets of the social structure in Israel. The second problem concerns the *change* in the political structure and in the relationships between political and social structure which may be inferred on the basis of such a description.

Clearly the description and analysis here of the political structure and its relationship to the social structure is fragmentary and falls very far short of meeting the desiderata listed previously. The opinion survey data cited have not yet been reported in sufficient detail either to permit their full exploitation or to evaluate their quality and importance. Both limitations of the "ecological correlations" approach itself and the grossness of the categories employed here in its application have been noted previously. Hopefully further and more detailed analysis of the 1961 census data in conjunction with the 1961 election data for Israel may overcome some of these limitations. Analysis over a much greater number of geographic units, each very much smaller and more homogeneous than those employed here, should narrow the gap between "ecological correlations" and "individual correlations," i.e., should render "ecological correlations" much better indicators of "individual correlations" than is the case for the data presented here. Be that as it may, in the final analysis no single study can establish the description of Israel's political structure on an empirical footing. Rather, what is called for is an empirical orientation on the part of those concerned with the investigation of the political structure of Israel and the building up of a fund of data, empirical analyses, and replicative studies.

With the exception of the data cited on intergenerational change in religious observance, all of the data reviewed or presented in this chapter are discrete in their time references. Moreover there are no corresponding earlier, "benchmark" data with which to make inferences about change. However fragmentary the data concerning recent social bases of the vote for the various parties and political trends, data bearing upon past demographic or social bases of the vote, of party identification, or of party support are entirely nonexistent.

In the data at hand *Mapai* appears not only as consistently the plurality political party, but as a party with appeal to the broadest range of "ideological types," and with broad "ethnic" appeal and support cutting across the Oriental-European and Veteran Settler-New Immigrant divisions in the population. To the extent that *Mapai* may previously have been a "movement" with a compact ideological package and a narrow basis of electoral support, then its present status as reflected in these data would seem to indicate that change has taken place in the direction of a broadening of its bases of support. Such a change may or may not have been contingent upon a dilution of *Mapai's* ideological offerings; and of course no data bearing upon this question are cited here.

Aside from *Mapai* only the Religious parties appear in these data to receive significant proportions of their popular support from both European born and Oriental population elements. Thus although the Religious parties have a core of European-born and Israel-born leaders and followers, from the data it would appear that they have obtained consider-able numbers of new supporters, perhaps comprising now a majority, from among the Oriental immigrant groups. But the trends towards diminishing religious observance—and perhaps the other changes in educational and socio-economic characteristics, some of which are discussed in the chapters which follow—may be operating to cut at the foundations of popular support for the Religious political parties among the Oriental immigrants.

Popular support for *Herut* appears to be confined to a considerable extent to the Oriental immigrant population groups; but within this category *Herut* enjoys broad support among the different "ideological types" (and also among "non-ideological" types) and among the different educational achievement groups. The Liberal party support appears to be confined to European-origin population elements; and within these groups its support appears to be centered in the better-educated groups and among the right-of-center "ideological types." Thus for the case of *Herut,* whose beginnings are in the European-originating Revisionist movement and in the prestatehood underground military organization, *Irgun Zvai Leumi,* it is probably not implausible to infer quite sweeping changes in the bases of its popular support. On the other hand, there is no obvious reason to infer greatly changing sources of support for the Liberal party.

Finally, the left-wing parties, *Mapam* and *Ahdut Avodah* are seen as groups with relatively little support, confined to left-wing "ideological types," rejected by the less-educated elements in the European-origin population, but getting some support from Oriental as well as European "better educated" groups. There appears nothing in the data concerning these groups which would lead to the inference of recent change in the social bases of such support as they receive. Again, it can only be hoped that additional data relating both to sources of support and to ideological orientations—and to their breadth, flexibility, or rigidity—will be added to permit more solidly-based analyses, interpretations, and inferences.

4

EDUCATION, MOBILITY, AND
CHANGES IN THE OCCUPATIONAL STRUCTURE

I. INTRODUCTION

IN THIS CHAPTER trends in occupational structure and in factors affecting occupational structure in Israel are considered. The social and economic processes associated with changing occupational and industrial structure in Israel are not only of importance for Israel herself; they also raise a number of more general questions concerning relationships between changes in social structure and changes in industrial structure associated with economic growth and development.

In the *Yishuv* (the pre-independence Jewish community in Palestine) two types of distinctions were typically made between sectors of the Jewish economy and between types of economically active persons: the "public" or "cooperative" sector as distinct from the "private sector" of the Jewish economy; and the "urban" as distinct from the "rural" or "agricultural" sectors of the economy. In addition a distinction was often made between "workers" and "non-workers"; but this distinction was primarily a political rather than an economic or social one. Professionals, self-employed tradesmen and craftsmen, members of cooperatives, clerks, and politicians could all be "workers" in the *Yishuv*. The criterion for being or not being a "worker" was "non-exploitation" of other workers and membership in or sympathy with a workers' organization, the General Federation of Labor, or a Labor Zionist political party.

Thus actual economic differentiation in the Jewish popu-

lation of pre-independence Palestine did not receive a great
deal of attention or publicity, though there is no reason to
presume that such differentiation did not exist. One reason
for lack of emphasis upon or attention to socio-economic
differences may have been the absence of groups, agencies,
or factions interested in using such differences as bases for
political appeals. Also the organizations of the Zionist enterprise usually felt it in the best interests of the community
to stress the unity and solidarity of the *Yishuv*—and not socio-
economic differences within the Jewish community. Similarly,
such "underdog" and underprivileged Jewish elements as
existed were typically not vociferous in their protests and
demands upon the rest of the community and were slow to
draw attention to their needs. Underprivileged persons are
everywhere characterized by low levels of "joining" or participation in voluntary organizations. So too in the *Yishuv*
the underprivileged elements were typically marginal to the
activities, the interests, and attention of the Zionist enterprise.[1] Moreover, these elements tended to be concentrated
in religious and traditional groups, and in these groups
poverty was an accepted way of life. Accordingly, few efforts
were made to organize such groups.

There were very many exceptions to the pattern of inatten-
tion to depressed or underprivileged groups. Many private
social welfare organizations (probably the best known of
which was and is *Hadassah*), and religious institutions were in
close touch with conditions among the less-well-off elements
of the Jewish population; and even certain Departments of the
Mandatory Government devoted attention to the health and
educational problems of these groups. However, real attention to the problem of educational and socio-economic level
differences came only in the wake of the mass immigration. In
the first place, the underprivileged immigrants were everywhere present and visible. In the second place, having immediately enjoyed full franchise, they became forthwith targets

1. S. N. Eisenstadt, "The Social Conditions of the Development of
Voluntary Associations . . . ," *op. cit.*

of agitation, organization, and vote solicitation. From the points of view both of the less prestigious and privileged and of the more prestigious and privileged groups, the relative differences were much more visible and the relative deprivations much more apparent. Finally, institutionalized concern for the welfare of all sectors of the population became part and parcel of public policy; and the responsibility of the newly independent Israel for the most elementary care and welfare of its citizens has never been seriously in question in Israel.

In Chapter 2 some of the disparities in socio-economic, occupational, and educational status between the different sectors of the Jewish population of Israel were listed. In the next section of the present chapter trends in literacy, knowledge of the Hebrew language, and levels of educational attainment are examined. In the following two sections changes in the patterns of labor force participation and occupational distribution are reviewed; and in the fifth and sixth sections patterns of intergenerational occupational mobility are plotted. In the final section the data of earlier sections are summarized with reference to changes in the occupational and industrial structure in Israel; and some more general implications of this analysis are noted.

II. LITERACY, KNOWLEDGE OF HEBREW, AND
EDUCATIONAL ATTAINMENT

In the November, 1948, registration of the Jewish population of Israel each person was asked whether or not he was literate (in any language and also, in particular, in Hebrew). Ninety-four percent of the Jewish population, including ninety-seven percent of the males and ninety percent of the females, reported themselves literate in some language. No literacy question was asked of a national sample of the population until the 1961 Census. However, educational attainment questions were asked on two national sample surveys in 1954 and 1957, and persons indicating that they had never attended any school at all were considered, for comparative purposes, not literate.

In Table 4.1 it is seen that the percentage literate in the population declined from 1948 to 1954 in the wake of the mass immigration. Unfortunately the change, if any, from 1954 to 1957 is not so clear, not only because the base populations are not comparable (i.e. persons 14+ in 1957, and persons 15+ in 1948 and 1954) but because certain comparisons conflict with one another. For example, the percentage literate among males declines, and the percentage literate among females increases; but the reasons for this contrast in directions of change are not obvious at all.

But it seems clear that since there is now free and compulsory primary school attendance in Israel to age fourteen, the percentage illiterate in the population must ordinarily tend to diminish and may be sustained only by increasing numbers of illiterate immigrants. Indeed, the increase in percent literate and in percent ever attending school is already discernible in the data obtained from the 1961 Census of Population (last two lines of Table 4.1).

A quite elaborate study of the revival of Hebrew as a spoken language in Palestine and in Israel has been carried

TABLE 4.1.

PERCENT LITERATE OR EVER ATTENDING SCHOOL AMONG JEWISH POPULATION OF ISRAEL, BY SEX, 1948-1961

YEAR	AGE GROUP	CHARACTERISTIC	TOTAL %	MALE %	FEMALE %
1948	15+	Percent Literate	93.7	96.8	90.4
1954	15+	Percent Ever Attending School	85.0	91.8	78.3
1957	14+	Percent Ever Attending School	85.6	90.9	80.4
1961	14+	Percent Ever Attending School	87.5	92.3	82.6
1961	14+	Percent Literate	88.0	92.9	83.0

Source: Israel Central Bureau of Statistics, *Statistical Abstract of Israel* No. 11, 1959-60, Part S, Table 31, p. 393; and No. 14, 1963, Part T, Table 38, p. 658.

out by R. Bachi.[2] According to Bachi's estimates, some twenty-six percent of the adult Jewish population (aged 15+) spoke Hebrew exclusively or as a first language in 1914, but by 1948 this had increased to about seventy percent. In the same period, the percentage of children aged two to fourteen speaking Hebrew as their only or first language rose from fifty-four percent to ninety-three percent. The percentages speaking Hebrew declined sharply subsequent to the mass immigration, but have been recovering steadily since. In December, 1950, the percentage of the adult population speaking Hebrew had declined to fifty-two percent; it rose to fifty-three percent in the middle of 1954; to fifty-eight percent in June, 1956; and to seventy-five percent by May, 1961.[3]

Using a variety of tables and indexes, Bachi plots and measures the associations between speaking Hebrew and other demographic and socio-economic attributes. The most important of these are age and sex, age at arrival in Israel (or Palestine), duration of residence in the country, working force participation, education abroad, and type of settlement.[4] Bachi concludes that, since 1. the Hebrew language has no effective competition as a spoken language among youth and children in Israel, and 2. the Hebrew language has become, for adults, the practical *lingua franca* of Israel and of Israeli social, economic, and political life, the "struggle for Hebrew" is basically already won in Israel.

In an earlier chapter it was noted that the new immigrants, and especially those from Oriental countries, arrived in Israel educationally "underprivileged" relative to veteran residents; and that the question of equality of educational opportunities, and hence of socio-economic opportunities, is often viewed as *the* social problem in Israel. Thus there would be particular interest in data bearing upon the extent to which educational

2. R. Bachi, "A Statistical Analysis of the Revival of Hebrew in Israel," in R. Bachi, (ed.), *Scripta Hierosolymitana*, Vol. III (Jerusalem: The Magnes Press, 1956).

3. CBS, *Statistical Abstract of Israel* No. 11, Part 5, Table 33, and No. 14, Part 7, Table 44.

4. Bachi, *op. cit.*

TABLE 4.2.

MEDIAN NUMBER OF SCHOOL YEARS COMPLETED AMONG JEWISH POPULATION AGED 14+, BY SEX, AGE GROUPS, AREA OF BIRTH, AND PERIOD OF IMMIGRATION—MAY 1961

	MALES					FEMALES				
	TOTAL	14-29	30-44	45-64	65+	TOTAL	14-29	30-44	45-64	65+
ALL PLACES OF BIRTH—TOTAL	8.9	9.4	8.6	8.6	7.4	7.9	9.1	7.7	7.3	3.9
Born in Israel—Total	10.7	10.9	10.1	9.3	8.5	10.4	10.8	9.7	7.3	1.0
Father Born in Israel	10.1	10.5	9.6	9.2	7.8	9.4	10.2	8.9	7.0	0.8
Father Born in Asia Africa	8.3	8.6	7.6	7.4	6.1	8.0	8.7	7.0	5.4	0.8
Father Born in Europe, America	11.4	11.4	11.4	10.5	10.9	11.4	11.5	11.3	8.6	5.9
Born in Asia, Africa—Total	6.9	7.7	6.8	5.5	2.5	3.7	6.7	1.4	0.7	0.6
Immigrated before 1948	7.2	8.2	7.6	6.6	4.2	3.6	7.7	5.6	0.8	0.6
Immigrated 1948-1954	6.9	7.6	6.8	5.2	2.2	3.3	6.6	1.0	0.7	0.6
Immigrated 1955 or after	6.8	7.7	6.2	5.0	1.2	5.0	6.7	1.2	0.7	0.6
Born in Europe, America—Total	9.5	9.9	9.4	9.5	8.4	8.8	9.8	8.8	8.7	6.4
Immigrated before 1948	10.4	10.6	10.2	10.6	9.9	9.6	10.6	9.7	9.7	7.6
Immigrated 1948-1954	8.6	9.8	8.6	8.0	7.2	8.0	9.7	8.2	7.4	5.3
Immigrated 1955 or after	8.9	9.9	9.0	8.4	7.8	8.6	10.1	8.7	7.9	6.4

Source: Israel Central Bureau of Statistics, *Monthly Statistical Bulletin, Part A*, Vol. 14, No. 11, Nov., 1963 *Supplement: Level of Education of the Population—Results of 1961 Census of Population*. Table 6, pp. 20-23

opportunities have become available to previously "underprivileged" sectors of the population. Some inferences about trends in educational opportunities may be attempted drawing upon a number of different kinds of data.

The 1961 census data on levels of school attainment permit comparison of educational attainment of successive broad age cohorts, and it is clear from Table 4.2 that the younger cohorts exhibit, on the whole, notably higher levels of educational attainment. On the other hand, comparison of the youngest adult cohorts, say aged fourteen to twenty-nine, born in Asia and Africa and in the Total Population respectively, shows that, even at the youngest ages, there were still in 1961 enormous differences in educational attainment for the different continent-of-birth groups. Differences within place-of-birth groups but between veteran-settler and new-immigrant subgroups are also apparent, though not so pronounced; and the veteran settlers at all ages enjoy higher levels of educational attainment than the new immigrants.

Some data on numbers of schools, teaching posts, and pupils for the 1948-1963 period are given in Table 4.3, and these may be compared to the growth of the school-age population shown in the same table. The numbers of pupils in secondary education, in vocational training, and in teacher training have grown faster than the school-age population; and, with the number of secondary school pupils increasing much more rapidly than population growth, the number of secondary school teaching posts has lagged. All in all, the data indicate a very remarkable growth of educational facilities and pupil enrollment in a very short time in Israel. In particular, according to Israel Central Bureau of Statistics estimates the percentage of Jewish youth aged fourteen to seventeen attending schools (attendance at primary schools is compulsory and free only to age fourteen) increased from forty-three percent in the 1951/52 school year to sixty-one percent in the 1961/62 school year.[5]

5. CBS, *Statistical Abstract* No. 11, Table 8, p. 380.

TABLE 4.3.

JEWISH POPULATION AGED 5-19, PUPILS, EDUCATIONAL INSTITUTIONS, AND TEACHING POSTS: NUMBER AND PERCENT CHANGE, 1948/49—1962/63

	1948/49	1962/63	PERCENT CHANGE
JEWISH POPULATION 5-19 YRS., TOTAL	177,986	668,212	275
5-9	57,565	234,656	308
10-14	60,461	239,978	297
15-19	59,960	193,578	223
PUPILS IN JEWISH EDUCATIONAL SYSTEM, TOTAL	127,470	563,383	353
Kindergartens	25,406	79,164	212
Primary Schools	91,133	380,396	317
Schools for Handicapped Children	—	9,418	—
Schools for Working Youth	—	5,394	—
Secondary (Day) Schools	6,411	40,425	531
Secondary Evening Schools	—	5,140	—
Continuation Classes	1,048	9,125	771
Vocational Schools	2,002	18,174	808
Agricultural Schools	—	7,441	—
Teachers' Training Colleges	1,470	7,064	381
Other Post-Primary Schools	—	1,642	—
INSTITUTIONS IN JEWISH EDUCATIONAL SYSTEM, TOTAL	1,286	4,146	222
Kindergartens	709	2,201	210
Primary Schools	467	1,188	154
Schools for Handicapped Children	—	106	—
Schools for Working Youth	—	138	—
Secondary (Day) Schools	39	132	228
Secondary Evening Schools	—	38	—
Continuation Classes	33	112	239
Vocational Schools	26	114	338
Agricultural Schools	—	44	—
Teachers' Training Colleges	12	38	217
Other Post-Primary Schools	—	35	—
TEACHING POSTS IN JEWISH EDUCATIONAL SYSTEM, TOTAL	6,283	29,966	377
Kindergartens	976	2,555	162
Primary Schools	4,153	17,841	330
Schools for Handicapped Children	—	947	—

TABLE 4.3 (Cont.)

	1948/49	1962/63	PERCENT CHANGE
Schools for Working Youth	—	342	—
Secondary (Day) Schools	704	2,892	311
Secondary Evening Schools	—	547	—
Continuation Classes	—	1,396	—
Vocational Schools	237	1,685	611
Agricultural Schools	—	689	—
Teachers' Training Colleges	213	944	343
Other Post-Primary Schools	—	128	—

Source: Israel Central Bureau of Statistics, *Statistical Abstract of Israel* No. 14, 1963, Part T, Table 1, 2, and 7.

But these data leave open the question of expansion of educational opportunities to all population sectors and in particular to the "educationally underprivileged" new immigrant and Oriental sectors. Data showing rates of school attendance or enrollment in the different population sectors have only recently been published. Table 4.4 shows rates per 1000 population of post-primary school attendance among youths aged fourteen to seventeen born in Israel, in Asia or Africa, and in Europe or America.

For the 1956/57 school year, the general attendance rate for Israel-born youths was 580, compared to 409 among those born in Europe or America and 130 among those born in Asia or Africa; and the rate for the entire population (all places of birth) was 352 per 1000 population. While the attendance rate for the population as a whole increased to 465 per 1000 by the 1961/62 school year, the rate for Israel-born youths climbed to 590. The attendance rate for European-born youths improved considerably, increasing to 550; but the rate for those born in Asia or Africa more than doubled in this period, increasing to 262 per 1000 population.

Considering now only those attending post-primary

TABLE 4.4.

RATES OF POST-PRIMARY SCHOOL ATTENDANCE AMONG JEWISH YOUTHS AGED 14-17, BY PLACE OF BIRTH AND TYPE OF SCHOOL (PER 1000 POPULATION), 1956/7 AND 1961/2

	PLACE OF BIRTH AND SCHOOL YEAR							
	1956/7				1961/2			
TYPE OF SCHOOL	Total	Israel	Asia-Africa	Europe-America	Total	Israel	Asia-Africa	Europe-America
All Post-Primary Schools	352.2	580.0	130.3	408.8	465.2	590.5	262.2	550.5
Secondary Day Schools	147.0	260.7	32.6	189.2	218.7	278.7	80.2	315.3
Secondary Evening Schools	24.7	32.3	15.4	33.6	26.3	28.8	27.0	21.4
Continuation Classes	56.3	101.4	15.7	57.1	47.6	88.6	14.9	30.1
Vocational Schools	58.6	96.8	22.0	65.9	80.3	98.8	48.9	94.8
Agricultural Schools	46.2	52.2	41.0	45.1	36.6	40.9	30.4	38.4
Teachers' Training Colleges	19.4	36.6	3.6	17.9	21.9	36.3	10.2	15.8
Other Post-Primary Schools	—	—	—	—	33.8	18.4	50.6	34.7

Source: Israel Central Bureau of Statistics, *Statistical Abstract of Israel* No. 14, 1963, Part T., Table 17, p. 642.

TABLE 4.5.

JEWISH POST-PRIMARY SCHOOL PUPILS BY PLACE OF BIRTH: PERCENT DISTRIBUTIONS BY TYPE OF SCHOOL 1956/57-1961/2

TYPE OF SCHOOL	ALL PLACES OF BIRTH			PLACE OF BIRTH AND SCHOOL YEAR BORN IN ISRAEL			BORN IN ASIA OR AFRICA			BORN IN EUROPE OR AMERICA		
	1956/7	1958/9	1961/2	1956/7	1958/9	1961/2	1956/7	1958/9	1961/2	1956/7	1958/9	1961/2
All Post-Primary Schools	100.0	100.0	100.0	100.0	100.0	100.0	100.0	100.0	100.0	100.0	100.0	100.0
Secondary Day Schools	42.3	45.2	48.1	45.7	48.8	48.0	25.0	30.9	32.2	46.6	46.6	58.2
Secondary Evening Schools	7.1	6.6	5.8	5.6	5.2	5.0	11.9	12.2	10.8	8.3	6.3	3.9
Continuation Classes	16.2	13.8	10.5	17.7	15.3	15.2	12.1	10.5	6.0	14.1	11.6	5.5
Vocational Schools	16.8	19.0	17.6	17.0	18.2	17.0	16.9	21.7	19.6	16.2	19.2	17.5
Agricultural Schools	13.3	9.5	8.0	9.2	6.0	7.1	31.5	19.1	12.3	11.2	12.0	7.2
Teachers' Training Colleges	4.3	5.9	4.1	4.8	6.5	5.3	2.6	5.6	3.3	3.6	4.3	2.5
Other Post-Primary Schools	—	—	5.9	—	—	2.4	—	—	15.8	—	—	5.2

Source: Supplement: Composition of Pupils in Hebrew Education by Place of Birth and Period of Immigration, 1956/7-1961/2, Table 10, pp. 14-15. Israel Central Bureau of Statistics, Monthly Statistical Bulletin, Part A, Vol. 14, No. 4, April 1963.

schools, it is seen in Table 4.5 that youths born in Asia and Africa differ radically from those born in Israel or in Europe or America with respect to the kinds of schools attended and the kind of post-primary education being obtained. Of Asian-African-born youths in post-primary schools, only twenty-five percent were attending secondary day schools in 1956/57, though this percentage increased to thirty-two percent by the 1961/62 school year. By contrast, among Israel-born post-primary school pupils aged fourteen to seventeen, about forty-six to forty-eight percent were pupils in secondary day schools; and of the fourteen to seventeen year old post-primary school pupils born in Europe or America, some forty-seven percent were pupils in secondary day schools in 1956/57, and this percentage increased to fifty-eight percent in secondary day schools in the 1961/62 school year.

Thus among youths aged fourteen to seventeen in the Jewish population, the rate of secondary day school attendance per 1000 born in Israel reached 279 by 1961/62; and the rate of secondary day school attendance per 1000 born in Europe or America reached 315 by 1961/62. But among youths fourteen to seventeen who were born in Asia or Africa, the rate of secondary day school attendance attained by 1961/62 was only eighty per 1000 population (Table 4.4).[6]

The changes or improvements not withstanding, the actual number of Oriental immigrant youths in the post-primary educational system, and especially in regular secondary day schools, remains absolutely and relatively small. While Asian-African born immigrants constituted thirty-five percent of the population aged fourteen to seventeen in 1961/62, they comprised only thirteen percent of the secondary day school

6. These and related data are discussed in more detail in CBS, *Monthly Statistical Bulletin,* Part A, Vol. 14, No. 4, April 1963, *Supplement: Composition of Pupils in Jewish Educational System by Place of Birth and Period of Immigration.* The discussion in this publication stresses the increase in the rate of post-primary school enrollments per 1000 population 14-17 born in Asia and Africa, rather than the place-of-birth differentials (though the latter are not ignored at all).

pupils in that school year. Even smaller is the percentage of university and other higher educational institution students who were born in Asia or Africa. There remains a kind of "sorting process" operating to steer Israel-born and European-born youths into post-primary, especially secondary, education in much larger proportions than is the case among Oriental youths. The same "sorting process" steers youths born in Asia and Africa directly into the labor force. This process still operates to exclude all but a very few of the Oriental youths from those social, economic, and political roles, benefits, opportunities, responsibilities, and style of life for which secondary education is in Israel, perhaps even more than elsewhere, an institutionalized prerequisite.

III. CHANGES IN PATTERNS OF LABOR FORCE PARTICIPATION

Although surveys of the labor force in Israel have been conducted by the Israel Central Bureau of Statistics since June 1954, unfortunately it is not yet possible to obtain reliable time series data for labor force characteristics in detail without performing adjustments and corrections. Procedures and definitions have been changed by the Bureau a number of times. These changes are not always adequately or precisely described in the Bureau's publications and it is sometimes impossible to avoid confounding the effects of procedural changes with changes in labor force characteristics in one or another subgroup of the population. Sampling variability has been an obstacle to detailed analysis of labor force components. Nevertheless, a number of observations are possible based upon the survey data for the years 1954-1961 which probably hold true regardless of the variations in quality of the data or of the procedures employed in any one year or in any one survey.

It seems clear that new immigrants had and continue to have lower rates of labor force participation than veteran

TABLE 4.6.

JEWISH POPULATION OF ISRAEL AGED 14+ BY SEX, PLACE OF BIRTH, AND DURATION OF RESI-
DENCE: LABOR FORCE PARTICIPATION RATES (PERCENT IN THE LABOR FORCE), 1954-1961

PLACE OF BIRTH, AND DURATION OF RESIDENCE	JUNE 1954	NOV. 1955	JUNE 1956	AVERAGE 1957	AVERAGE 1958	AVERAGE 1959	AVERAGE 1960	AVERAGE 1961
BOTH SEXES:								
Total—All Places of Birth	49.4	54.4	52.2	55.3	54.5	53.9	54.1	54.4
Born in Israel	43.5	51.8	47.5	53.1	50.5	50.7	49.7	52.7
Born in Europe-America								
Veteran Residents	60.3	61.7	60.6	62.7	61.7	61.8	62.8	61.6
New Immigrants	51.6	54.4	52.6	56.2	56.3	55.7	55.1	54.7
Born in Asia-Africa								
Veteran Residents	50.2	52.9	49.4	56.3	52.5	50.2	53.6	53.9
New Immigrants	43.8	47.9	46.5	48.0	48.6	48.8	49.2	50.2
MALES:								
Total—All Places of Birth	76.6	80.3	78.5	79.9	79.3	79.5	73.4	79.0
Born in Israel	59.1	64.9	61.5	66.1	62.9	64.2	62.5	67.1

144

Born in Europe-America								
Veteran Residents	91.5	91.0	89.5	90.5	89.3	89.5	89.1	88.9
New Immigrants	83.8	81.2	81.6	82.8	82.4	82.4	80.3	79.5
Born in Asia-Africa								
Veteran Residents	83.2	81.6	79.8	86.0	84.6	83.4	85.2	82.8
New Immigrants	74.5	76.3	73.9	73.9	75.7	77.0	76.0	77.4
FEMALES:								
Total—All Places of Birth	21.7	27.9	25.3	30.4	29.4	28.0	29.5	29.4
Born in Israel	27.4	37.4	32.6	39.3	37.8	36.2	36.8	38.2
Born in Europe-America								
Veteran Residents	27.9	31.2	29.6	33.9	32.7	32.9	34.1	32.8
New Immigrants	21.5	28.3	25.5	31.2	30.9	29.7	32.0	30.6
Born in Asia-Africa								
Veteran Residents	15.2	21.9	18.2	22.9	(18.0)	17.8	19.2	21.5
New Immigrants	14.8	19.9	18.6	21.4	21.3	20.5	22.2	22.7

Source: 1955, 1957, 1958, 1959, 1960, 1961—Israel Central Bureau of Statistics, *Statistical Abstracts, No. 10, 11,* 1954: *LF Survey, June, 1954,* Table 7, p. 13; 1956: *LF Survey, June,* 1956, Table 11, pp. 22-23.

settlers (Table 4.6). One important exception to this pattern
is for female Oriental new immigrants, whose rate of labor
force participation (23% in 1961) is similar to that of female
veteran settlers of Asian and African birth (22% in 1961).
But in general European new immigrants have lower labor
force participation rates than European veteran settlers; Oriental new immigrants have lower labor force participation
rates than Oriental veteran settlers; and both males and
females of the Oriental community, new immigrants or veteran
settlers, have lower rates of labor force participation than the
European male and female groups. These comparisons hold,
with the exception noted, for the entire 1954-1961 period.

Oriental immigrant women have low labor force participation rates regardless of duration of residence. On the
other hand, women born in Israel have particularly high labor
force participation rates especially in view of the fact that
even the "adult" (aged 14+) population is very young. While
the males born in Israel are characterized by lower labor
force participation rates than any of the immigrant groups,
mostly because of the "youthfulness" of the born-in-Israel
group, the females born in Israel have *higher* rates of labor
force participation than any of the immigrant groups of
females *despite* a similar "youthfulness." Thus the 1954-61
Labour Force Survey data do indicate a certain stable pattern
of labor force participation in the various subgroups of the
population, but they do not offer many clues with respect to
changes occurring or likely to occur in extent of labor force
participation.

Labor force participation rates for women aged eighteen
to thirty-four and thirty-five to fifty-four respectively, by
continent of birth and duration of residence are given in the
top two panels of Table 4.7 for the years 1957-1961. Since
both veteran settlers and new immigrant women of Asian
and African birth are characterized by low labor force participation rates, it is often held that non-participation of
women in the labor force is a characteristic of the Oriental
communities, independent of duration of residence in Israel,

and not likely to change much in the future.[7] However, such a conclusion seems somewhat premature; nonparticipation of Oriental women in the labor force is surely related both to their low levels of education and the high levels of fertility, both of which show some signs of changing.[8]

Labor force participation rates of Oriental new immigrant males aged fifty-five to sixty-four have been lower than for other groups the same age, and unemployment rates for the same group have been chronically high (Table 4.7, third panel). The low labor force participation and high unemployment reflect chronic difficulties for the large numbers of unskilled persons in this group in obtaining and holding employment. Being unskilled, relatively inexperienced in the local labor market, ordinarily not fluent in Hebrew, often not literate in any language, and not as strong physically as, say, younger competing unskilled workers, Oriental male immigrants this age have often withdrawn altogether from the labor force (i.e., have stopped seeking employment and hence are, by definition, "not in the labor force"). This chronic locus of low labor force participation is generally recognized as one type of unemployment, and the actual unemployment rates of those in the labor force have always been high. But these labor force participation rates are likely to increase as the age-group is progressively filled by persons who had immigrated at younger ages and had been absorbed in employment prior to reaching age fifty-five. Indeed, there is considerable indication that such an increase in labor force participation rate for this group has already begun.

Finally, the labor force participation rates for youths and adolescents aged fourteen to seventeen are subject to change in the wake of possible changes in education laws

7. See for example, "Project Report No. 1: The Labour Force in Israel," in Falk Project for Economic Research, *Fifth Report, 1959-60* (Jerusalem: Falk Project, 1961).

8. *Cf.* R. Bachi and J. Matras, "Contraception and Induced Abortions among Jewish Maternity Cases in Israel," *op. cit.;* and J. Matras and C. Auerbach, "On Rationalization of Family Formation in Israel," *op. cit.*

TABLE 4.7.

JEWISH POPULATION OF ISRAEL: LABOR FORCE PARTICIPA-
TION RATES FOR SELECTED AGE-SEX GROUPS, BY PLACE OF
BIRTH AND DURATION OF RESIDENCE, 1957-1961

AGE—SEX GROUP PLACE OF BIRTH, AND DURATION OF RESIDENCE	YEAR				
	1957	1958	1959	1960	1961
FEMALES, 18-34:					
Born in Israel	50.8	50.9	48.5	48.3	49.8
Born in Europe-America					
Veteran Residents	40.7	39.5	36.1	40.2	37.3
New Immigrants	38.0	40.4	37.6	37.1	39.5
Born in Asia-Africa					
Veteran Residents	(28.0)	(28.2)	(23.4)	(25.1)	(27.6)
New Immigrants	27.0	24.9	25.4	28.4	28.9
FEMALES, 35-54:					
Born in Israel	(27.7)	(24.8)	(21.3)	(34.6)	(35.5)
Born in Europe-America					
Veteran Residents	37.1	36.0	37.2	37.7	37.6
New Immigrants	35.1	31.9	32.8	37.0	35.7
Born in Asia-Africa					
Veteran Residents	(22.0)	(15.7)	(16.7)	(20.5)	(25.7)
New Immigrants	15.2	15.9	15.3	17.5	17.3
MALES, 55-64:					
Born in Europe-America					
Veteran Residents	94.4	92.6	94.0	93.2	93.1
New Immigrants	85.7	87.1	87.2	88.2	88.6
Born in Asia-Africa					
New Immigrants	59.4	61.3	62.8	68.7	72.3
MALES, 14-17:					
Born in Israel	33.8	26.0	27.9	26.5	34.7
Born in Europe-America					
New Immigrants	(35.5)	(38.1)	(32.4)	(16.6)	(31.4)
Born in Asia-Africa					
New Immigrants	43.4	42.6	42.7	36.3	45.0

Source: Israel Central Bureau of Statistics, *Statistical Abstracts, Nos. 10,
11, 12, 13*, 1958-59, 1959-60, 1960-61, and 1962.

and opportunities. (See Table 4.7 bottom panel.) At the present time, the fourteen to seventeen year age period is that between compulsory primary school attendance and compulsory military service, so that labor force attachments, when they exist, tend to have a temporary or casual nature at this age. The instability of labor force attachments at this age is also reflected in the highest unemployment rates for any group occurring at this age. Thus either a compulsory post-primary school attendance law and/or availability of free secondary or other post-primary educational opportunities in the near future would alter the extent of labor force participation of persons this age.

IV. CHANGES IN THE OCCUPATIONAL DISTRIBUTION

The sampling variability, procedural changes, and definitional changes in collection and publication of the labor force sample survey statistics operate to limit the scope and detail of possible study of change in occupational distribution of the labor force in Israel. Nevertheless, certain trends can be discerned, if only over very brief time intervals, and it is of some interest to try to plot their directions and implications.

Between 1955 and 1961, certain changes in employment by major occupational category are evident, these distributional changes occurring mostly as a consequence of differential growth in the different economic branches, with very little absolute decline occurring.[9] For male employment the important changes are increases in industrial and crafts employment, with slight relative decrease in construction, substantial relative decrease in employment in commerce, banking, etc., and some decrease in employment in personal services. The fluctuation in agricultural employment reflects in part the role of the agricultural sector in absorption of immigrants, and future growth or decline of this sector is

-9. CBS, *Statistical Abstract of Israel*, No. 13, Part Q, Tables 5-7, pp. 388-93.

likely to be dependent very much upon the magnitude, composition, educational levels, and occupational skills of future waves of immigration.

For males employment in professional and technical occupations, in construction and industrial occupations (mostly industrial) and in service occupations has increased relative to the total. Employment in administrative and clerical occupations, in agricultural occupations, in transport and communications occupations, and especially in sales occupations and in unskilled industrial and construction occupations has declined relative to the total. For females, employment in service has increased while employment in agricultural and in sales occupations has decreased relative to the total.

Data on change in occupational distribution for the different sectors of the population are available for 1958 and 1961, and these are presented in Table 4.8. For Israel-born males the major changes are relative increases in professional and technical and in industrial and crafts employment, and decreases in other white collar, utility service, and agricultural employment. For male European-born veteran settlers relative increases in professional employment, and relative decreases in agricultural employment, decreases in transport employment, and service employment are evident. For new immigrants of European origin relative decreases in administrative and agricultural employment, and increases in professional and industrial employment are apparent. Among Oriental new immigrants employment in agriculture has diminished substantially as has employment in commerce; notable increases have taken place in industrial and crafts employment, and some increase in transport and in government and business services employment has taken place.

From 1955 through 1961, the percentage of employed males who were wage and salary workers increased from sixty-five percent to seventy-two percent, and the percentage of employers, self-employed, or members of cooperatives declined from twenty-six percent in 1955 to twenty-three percent in 1961 (the residual accounted for by members of collective settlements and unpaid family workers) despite the increase in this period in the number of self-employed *moshav* (small-holders' cooperative farm village) members.[10] The increase in the proportion of wage and salary workers combined with the data on changes in employment in the various sectors and occupational groups suggest certain very important developments in the structure of the labor force and of employment in Israel: evidently an increasing proportion of the labor force is organized in or associated with the growing industrial sector of the economy, and the proportion engaged in petty entrepreneurial activities, e.g., peddling and hawking, kiosk operation, self-employed tradesmen, etc., is declining. Although in some countries the decline of "business and commerce" sectors of employment may reflect a "downgrading" of the labor force, in Israel it reflects an "upgrading" of the labor force, the industrial employees representing skills, literacy levels, and economic security not typical in the petty business activities experiencing a relative decline.

V. INTERGENERATIONAL OCCUPATIONAL MOBILITY

Data relating to intergenerational occupational mobility and to changes in the occupational distributions associated with intergenerational mobility are available. The latter refer to Jewish grooms marrying in 1955 and include information for grooms reporting both their own and their fathers' occupations.[11]

The left panel of Table 4.9 gives the occupational distribution of employed persons—males *and* females—by age in June, 1954, and these are the only data available which are comparable to the separate data for grooms and their fathers for 1955. The latter, shown in the right hand panel of Table 4.9, give occupational distributions for the grooms and their

10. *Ibid.*, Table 10, pp. 398-9.
11. J. Matras, "Some Data on Intergenerational Occupational Mobility in Israel," *Population Studies*, XVII, No. 2 (Nov., 1963).

TABLE 4.8.

JEWISH EMPLOYED PERSONS, TOTAL AND MALES, BY PLACE OF BIRTH—PERCENT DISTRIBUTION BY MAJOR OCCUPATION GROUPS: ISRAEL, 1955-1961

MAJOR OCCUPATION GROUPS	NOV. 1955	TOTAL—ALL PLACES OF BIRTH AVERAGE				
		1957	1958	1959	1960	1961
BOTH SEXES						
Percent	100.0	100.0	100.0	100.0	100.0	100.0
Professional and Technical Workers	10.9	11.7	11.3	11.3	11.9	12.3
Managers, Administrators, and Clerks	16.8	16.1	16.4	14.7	14.9	14.2
Merchants and Salesmen	11.7	10.7	9.1	9.0	9.3	8.9
Agricultural Workers	14.4	14.0	15.6	13.9	14.8	14.4
Transport and Communication Workers	6.1	4.8	5.0	4.7	4.9	4.7
Industrial and Building Workers and Craftsmen:						
Skilled and Semi-skilled	} 29.1	25.3	25.3	27.2	27.7	29.6
and Unskilled		5.8	5.5	5.9	3.6	3.0
Service Workers	11.0	11.6	11.8	12.9	12.9	12.9
MALES						
Percent	100.0	100.0	100.0	100.0	100.0	100.0
Professional and Technical Workers	7.3	7.9	8.1	8.4	8.9	9.3
Managers, Administrators, and Clerks	16.7	15.9	16.0	14.4	14.8	13.7
Merchants and Salesmen	11.3	10.3	8.9	8.5	8.9	8.5
Agricultural Workers	15.6	14.7	16.2	14.9	15.3	14.7
Transport and Communication Workers	8.0	6.4	6.6	5.9	6.4	6.1
Industrial and Building Workers and Craftsmen:						
Skilled and Semi-skilled	} 34.1	30.4	30.5	32.8	33.6	35.7
and Unskilled		7.1	6.6	6.8	4.2	3.6
Service Workers	7.1	7.3	7.1	8.3	7.9	8.4

MAJOR OCCUPATION GROUPS	BORN IN ISRAEL		BORN IN EUROPE-AMERICA				BORN IN ASIA-AFRICA			
			Veteran Settlers		New Immigrants		Veteran Settlers		New Immigrants	
	1958	1961	1958	1961	1958	1961	1958	1961	1958	1961
BOTH SEXES										
Percent	100.0	100.0	100.0	100.0	100.0	100.0	100.0	100.0	100.0	100.0
Prof. and Tech. Workers	18.5	22.5	14.3	17.4	11.1	12.0	(6.2)	(6.2)	3.9	3.9
Man., Admin., and Clerks	21.4	21.5	23.6	22.3	13.7	11.8	(13.8)	(11.8)	7.5	6.2
Merchants and Salesmen	(4.6)	(3.1)	10.9	11.8	10.7	11.8	(17.1)	(16.0)	5.9	5.9
Agricultural Workers	16.4	14.2	10.4	9.3	12.7	11.1	(8.5)	(6.0)	26.9	22.3
Trans. and Comm. Workers	7.8	7.5	5.8	5.1	4.7	4.2	(8.4)	(6.0)	(1.9)	3.0
Indus. and Build. Workers and Craftsmen: *Skilled and Semi-skilled and Unskilled*	22.5	22.8	26.0	25.4	33.9	35.4	32.7	32.8	38.6	41.0
Service Workers	8.8	8.4	9.0	8.7	13.2	13.7	(13.3)	(15.6)	15.3	17.7
MALES										
Percent	100.0	100.0	100.0	100.0	100.0	100.0	100.0	100.0	100.0	100.0
Prof. and Tech. Workers	11.4	15.2	11.1	14.9	8.2	9.3	(4.3)	(4.4)	(3.1)	(2.9)
Man., Admin., and Clerks	17.9	16.9	25.2	24.2	13.3	11.4	(12.6)	(12.0)	7.4	6.4
Merchants and Salesmen	(5.1)	(3.2)	10.2	10.8	9.8	10.6	(18.9)	(17.3)	6.5	6.0
Agricultural Workers	18.6	16.8	10.1	8.3	13.0	10.4	(8.6)	(11.3)	28.1	23.3
Trans. and Comm. Workers	11.7	10.7	7.7	6.7	6.1	5.8	(10.0)	(7.0)	2.4	3.6
Indus. and Build. Workers and Craftsmen: *Skilled and Semi-skilled and Unskilled*	30.7	32.6	30.3	30.6	41.3	43.7	37.1	36.9	43.9	45.5
Service Workers	4.6	(4.6)	5.4	4.5	8.3	8.8	(8.5)	(11.1)	8.6	12.3

Source: Israel Central Bureau of Statistics, *Statistical Abstract of Israel, No. 13*, Jerusalem, 1962, Part Q, Table 9, p. 397, and Table 13, p. 403.

153

TABLE 4.9.

EMPLOYED JEWISH MALES BY AGE GROUPS, ISRAEL, JUNE, 1954; JEWISH GROOMS MARRYING IN ISRAEL, 1955, AND GROOMS' FATHERS: DISTRIBUTIONS (PERCENT) BY BROAD OCCUPATION GROUPS

OCCUPATION GROUP	EMPLOYED PERSONS, JUNE, 1954: AGE GROUPS[a]								GROOMS, 1955, & FATHERS[b]	
	TOTAL	14-19	20-24	25-34	35-44	45-54	55-64	65+	GROOMS	GROOMS' FATHERS
Total: Number	474,000	31,000	54,900	125,700	116,300	95,000	38,500	12,000	13,467	5,877
Percent	100.0	100.0	100.0	100.0	100.0	100.0	100.0	100.0	100.0	100.0
Professional, Technical, Management	13.2	4.8	12.9	12.0	13.9	14.7	16.9	14.8	9.6	10.3
Clerical and Sales	23.9	15.1	19.1	19.6	23.6	30.0	32.1	40.0	15.3	34.5
Skilled and Semi-skilled	36.7	45.2	40.0	40.8	36.2	31.7	28.4	29.6	47.8	27.5
Unskilled	15.5	15.4	15.2	16.5	16.8	14.3	13.7	9.5	15.4	17.6
Farm	10.7	19.5	12.8	11.1	9.5	9.3	8.9	6.1	11.9	10.1

a. Source: Israel Central Bureau of Statistics, *Labor Force Survey, June 1954*, Jerusalem, 1957.
b. Source: Israel Central Bureau of Statistics, unpublished marriage data for 1955.

fathers. Both the 1954 *Labour Force Survey* data and sons-and-fathers 1955 marriage certificate data are consistent with each other in so far as both highlight the remarkable differences in occupational distribution by age. The younger groups are characterized by high proportions in skilled and semi-skilled occupations and in agricultural occupations and notably low proportions in clerical, commercial, and sales occupations. Older groups are characterized by high proportions in clerical, sales, and commercial occupations and low proportions in skilled and semi-skilled occupations. Again, the clerical, commercial, and sales occupations, far from representing pillars of white collar security and solidity, are in Israel often occupations in insecure small-scale retailing, one-person establishments such as kiosks, self-employed craftsmen and artisans, etc. On the other hand, the skilled and semi-skilled workers are typically organized in strong trade unions, benefit from employment security and a variety of welfare provisions, and

TABLE 4.10.

JEWISH GROOMS, ISRAEL, 1955, BY OWN OCCUPATION GROUPS AND BY FATHERS' OCCUPATION GROUPS (PERCENT DISTRIBUTION)

FATHERS' OCCUPATION GROUPS		SONS' (GROOMS') OCCUPATION GROUPS				
	TOTAL	PROF., TECH., MANAGE-MENT	CLERI-CAL SALES	SKILLED SEMI-SKILLED	UN-SKILLED	FARM
Total: Number	5,877	553	717	2,663	734	951
Percent	100.0	100.0	100.0	100.0	100.0	100.0
Professional, Technical, Management	10.3	33.3	11.7	6.7	4.1	7.5
Clerical, Sales	34.5	47.2	56.9	30.4	23.0	28.7
Skilled, Semi-skilled	27.5	12.0	18.0	39.2	19.5	17.1
Unskilled	17.6	3.5	9.3	18.4	49.9	8.5
Farm	10.1	4.0	4.1	5.3	3.5	38.2

Source: Israel Central Bureau of Statistics, unpublished marriage data for 1955.

are by and large both more secure and more affluent than are large numbers of marginal "businessmen" and "white collar" employees.

The social origins of the younger workers in the different occupational categories, at least in so far as these origins are reflected in the father's occupations, are shown in Table 4.10. It is important to remember that Israel's occupational structure has always been rather lopsided relative to those of other countries, Israel having relatively small proportions especially in agricultural, but also in manual occupations. As a consequence, while in most countries each occupation group has fairly large proportions of persons with farm origins, in Israel even in the farmer-group less than half come from farm origins, and almost a third of the bridegrooms in agricultural occupations are sons of fathers in non-manual occupations.

Persons in professional and technical occupations are recruited mostly from among the sons of non-manual fathers, with a third reporting their fathers also in professional and technical occupations, and almost half (47%) reporting fathers in clerical, commercial, and sales occupations. Sons in clerical, commercial, and sales occupations are also recruited, to a considerable extent, from among those whose fathers are in non-manual occupations, but twenty-seven percent reported their fathers in manual occupations, and four percent in agricultural pursuits. By contrast no less than thirty-seven percent of the younger (grooms) skilled and semi-skilled occupation groups are sons of fathers in non-manual occupations, and even twenty-seven percent of those in unskilled occupations are sons of white collar fathers; but a full fifty percent of the younger persons in unskilled occupations are sons of fathers in unskilled occupations as well. Again, the number of persons in Israel with "farm origins" is small, so that sons of farmers never comprise more than about five percent in any occupation group except agriculture. Even in agriculture the farmers' sons are outnumbered almost two to one by sons of non-manual and manual workers.

TABLE 4.11.

JEWISH GROOMS, ISRAEL, 1955, BY FATHERS' OCCUPATION GROUPS AND BY OWN OCCUPATION GROUPS (PERCENT DISTRIBUTION)

FATHERS' OCCUPATION GROUPS	SONS' (GROOMS') OCCUPATION GROUPS						
	PROF., TECH., MANAGEMENT	CLERICAL, SALES	SKILLED, SEMI-SKILLED	UN-SKILLED	FARM	TOTAL	NUMBER
Professional, Technical, Management	33.82	15.43	32.16	5.39	13.20	100.0	538
Clerical, Sales	13.56	21.18	42.20	8.82	14.24	100.0	1,917
Skilled, Semi-skilled	4.42	8.25	67.57	9.23	10.53	100.0	1,539
Unskilled	1.95	6.44	47.91	35.80	7.90	100.0	1,025
Farm	3.82	5.03	23.96	4.51	62.68	100.0	576
Number	552	711	2,651	733	948		5,595
Occupational Distributions:							
Fathers	9.62	34.26	27.51	18.32	10.29	100.0	
Sons (Grooms)	9.87	12.71	47.38	13.10	16.94	100.0	

Source: Israel Central Bureau of Statistics, unpublished marriage data for 1955.

The percent distributions of sons by occupation category is given in Table 4.11 for each group by occupation category of the fathers. The first noteworthy aspect of the table is how *few* of the sons reported being in the *same* occupation categories as their fathers. Almost two-thirds (65%) of the sons of skilled and semi-skilled fathers report themselves in the same category, and three-fifths (61%) of the farmers' sons are themselves farmers; but sons both of unskilled worker fathers and of fathers in clerical, sales, and commercial occupations are more likely to be in the skilled or semi-skilled occupation category than in their fathers' occupational category; and sons of professional and technical persons are as likely to be in skilled and semi-skilled occupations as in *their* fathers' occupational category. Altogether, forty-three percent of the sons reported themselves in the same occupational categories as their fathers, and fifty-seven percent reported themselves in different categories.

In order to compare the extent of intergenerational occupational mobility in Israel to that of other countries, the occupational categories have been consolidated in Table 4.12 to three categories: Manual, Non-manual, and Farm; and the proportion mobile computed on the basis of these three categories is comparable to proportions mobile computed for other countries based upon data given by Lipset and Bendix.[12]

It is clear from Table 4.12 that the high proportion mobile in Israel is itself rather unusual among the industrialized countries. Moreover, the directions of the mobility are most unusual: not only does the proportion in agriculture not diminish—it actually increases somewhat. The white collar occupations, enjoying such a boom in other countries, are diminishing in Israel or, at least, are not attracting the sons of the present incumbents of white collar roles; and the skilled and semi-skilled occupations attract sons of all occupational origins.

12. S. M. Lipset and R. Bendix, *Social Mobility in Industrial Society* (Berkeley: University of California Press, 1959) pp. 19-21.

TABLE 4.12.

INTERGENERATIONAL OCCUPATIONAL MOBILITY TABLES;
ISRAEL AND SELECTED INDUSTRIALIZED COUNTRIES:
OCCUPATIONAL DISTRIBUTIONS (PERCENT) OF SONS, BY
FATHERS' OCCUPATION GROUPS

COUNTRY AND FATHERS' OCCUPATION GROUPS	SONS' OCCUPATION GROUPS			
	NON-MANUAL	MANUAL	FARM	PROPORTION MOBILE
ISRAEL:				
Non-manual	38.0	48.0	14.0	
Manual	10.9	79.6	9.5	.579
Farm	8.8	28.5	62.7	
FRANCE:				
Non-manual	73.0	18.0	9.0	
Manual	35.0	55.0	10.0	.316
Farm	16.0	13.0	71.0	
GERMANY:				
Non-manual	58.0	38.0	4.0	
Manual	27.0	68.0	5.0	.349
Farm	19.0	28.0	54.0	
SWEDEN:				
Non-manual	74.0	23.0	3.0	
Manual	29.0	64.0	7.0	.439
Farm	23.0	42.0	35.0	
SWITZERLAND:				
Non-manual	84.0	13.0	3.0	
Manual	44.0	54.0	2.0	.307
Farm	27.0	19.0	54.0	
U.S.A.:				
Non-manual	64.0	34.0	1.0	
Manual	31.0	67.0	2.0	.464
Farm	24.0	46.0	30.0	
JAPAN:				
Non-manual	74.0	21.0	5.0	
Manual	33.0	59.0	8.0	.398
Farm	28.0	22.0	50.0	

Source: Israel, Table 4.11; other countries, S. M. Lipset and R.
Bendix, *Social Mobility in Industrial Society*, Berkeley, 1959, pp. 19-21.

VI. INTERGENERATIONAL OCCUPATIONAL MOBILITY:
   ETHNIC GROUP AND DURATION OF RESIDENCE COMPARISONS

Turning now to comparison of intergenerational occupational mobility patterns for the geo-cultural origin and duration-of-residence subgroups the percentages of sons of fathers in each occupation category moving to the various own-occupation categories are given in Table 4.13 for the different population sectors. New immigrants from Europe are characterized by the greatest amount of change both from the point of view of relative change in occupational distribution and from the point of view of the proportion among the sons in occupations different from those of their fathers (63%). The *least* amount of change in occupational distribution occurred for Oriental new immigrants. Nevertheless, a substantial percentage of the sons (57%) reported themselves in occupation categories different from those of their fathers. The extent of father-to-son change in occupational distributions among the Israel-born group was similar to that of the Oriental immigrant groups, but the proportion actually mobile among the Israel-born was notably lower, and lowest of all the groups.[13]

The intergenerational change in occupational distribution was less for European veteran settlers than for new immigrants, and a slightly larger proportion was mobile among the new immigrants (63% compared to 60% among veteran settlers). Among Oriental immigrants the percentages reporting mobility relative to fathers' occupation categories were about the same for new immigrants and veteran settlers, but the change in occupational distribution was slightly greater for the veteran settlers than for new immigrants. But, in

13. The proportion mobile is computed $P = 1 - \Sigma a_i p_{ii}$ where a_i = proportion of fathers in i-th occupation category, p_{ii} = proportion of sons of fathers in i-th category who remain in i-th category. See J. Matras, "Differential Fertility, Intergenerational Occupational Mobility, and Change in Occupational Distribution . . . ," *Population Studies*, XV, No. 2. (Nov., 1961).

general, the duration-of-residence differences in *amount* of changes seem too small to be of much significance.

Perhaps the most interesting comparisons between the ethnic and duration-of-residence subgroups are those concerned with *directions* of intergenerational change. These differences are so numerous as to defy summary and are best studied in detailed cell-by-cell comparison of the mobility tables of Table 4.13. Nevertheless, some of the most important differences may be pointed out.

1. For any given category of occupational origin, European- and Israel-born sons are much more likely to enter the professional and technical occupational category than are Oriental immigrants. European veteran settlers and Israel-born sons are more likely to enter this category than are European new immigrant sons, and Oriental veteran settler sons are more likely to enter this occupational category than new immigrant sons.

2. For any given category of occupational origin, Oriental new immigrant sons are much more likely to be in the unskilled occupational category than are sons from any of the other groups. European veteran settler and Israel-born sons are least likely to enter unskilled occupations: even European veteran settler and Israel-born sons of unskilled workers are not likely to be unskilled workers themselves (only 12% and 11% respectively). But European new immigrant and Oriental veteran settler sons of unskilled workers are fairly likely to enter unskilled occupations (22% and 27% respectively); and Oriental new immigrant sons of unskilled workers are very likely to remain unskilled workers, fifty-one percent reporting themselves unskilled workers. Among European-born, Israel-born, and Oriental veteran settler sons, very few are recruited to ranks of unskilled occupations *except* actual sons of unskilled workers. But Oriental new immigrant sons are recruited in large numbers to unskilled occupations regardless of category of origin.

3. Skilled and semi-skilled occupations both attract sons of all categories of fathers in all ethnic and duration-of-resi-

TABLE 4.13.

INTERGENERATIONAL OCCUPATIONAL MOBILITY TABLES: ISRAEL, JEWISH GROOMS MARRYING IN 1955, BY PLACE OF BIRTH AND DURATION OF RESIDENCE[a]

PLACE OF BIRTH, DURATION OF RESIDENCE, AND FATHERS' OCCUPATION GROUP	SONS' (GROOMS') OCCUPATION GROUP						SONS DISTRIBUTION BY FATHERS OCCUPATION GROUP		SONS PROPORTION MOBILE
	Total	Prof., Tech., Manage-ment	Cleri-cal, Sales	Skilled, Semi-Skilled	Un-skilled	Farm	N	%	
BORN IN ISRAEL:									
Total	100.00	12.25	13.09	50.59	3.27	20.78	1,429	100.00	.534
Prof., Tech., etc.	100.00	39.09	12.18	34.01	1.52	13.20	197	13.79	
Clerical, Sales	100.00	14.65	23.02	46.29	3.95	12.09	430	30.09	
Skilled, Semi-skilled	100.00	4.62	10.99	72.09	1.76	10.55	455	31.84	
Unskilled	100.00	1.50	6.77	62.41	11.28	18.05	133	9.31	
Farm	100.00	5.61	2.34	21.50	1.87	68.69	214	14.98	
BORN IN EUROPE-AMERICA:									
Total	100.00	14.05	16.01	49.61	5.87	14.46	2,199	100.00	.614
Prof., Tech., etc.	100.00	37.30	17.46	29.37	3.17	12.70	252	11.44	
Clerical, Sales	100.00	17.05	22.63	40.42	4.00	15.89	950	43.05	
Skilled, Semi-skilled	100.00	6.16	7.94	70.66	4.86	10.37	617	28.07	
Unskilled	100.00	3.69	9.96	60.52	18.82	7.01	271	12.31	
Farm	100.00	4.59	15.60	30.28	1.83	47.71	109	5.13	

VETERAN RESIDENTS:									
Total	100.00	17.03	19.34	48.50	3.11	12.02	998	100.00	.601
Prof., Tech., etc.	100.00	40.00	17.86	30.71	1.43	10.00	140	14.03	
Clerical, Sales	100.00	20.04	25.93	40.96	1.96	11.11	459	45.99	
Skilled, Semi-skilled	100.00	5.64	10.15	71.80	3.38	9.02	266	26.65	
Unskilled	100.00	5.62	14.61	56.18	12.36	11.24	89	8.92	
Farm	100.00	4.55	20.45	27.27		47.73	44	4.41	
NEW IMMIGRANTS:									
Total	100.00	11.64	13.17	50.47	8.24	16.48	1,177	100.00	.626
Prof., Tech., etc.	100.00	34.86	16.51	27.52	5.50	15.60	109	9.26	
Clerical, Sales	100.00	14.32	19.50	39.83	6.02	20.33	482	40.95	
Skilled, Semi-skilled	100.00	6.45	6.16	59.79	6.16	11.44	341	28.97	
Unskilled	100.00	2.78	7.78	62.78	21.67	5.00	180	15.29	
Farm	100.00	4.62	12.30	32.31	3.08	47.69	65	5.52	
BORN IN ASIA-AFRICA:									
Total	100.00	3.46	8.74	42.55	28.32	16.93	1,967	100.00	.578
Prof., Tech., etc.	100.00	12.36	16.85	35.95	20.22	14.61	89	4.52	
Clerical, Sales	100.00	6.52	17.13	42.09	21.23	13.04	537	27.27	
Skilled, Semi-skilled	100.00	1.92	6.00	59.10	22.27	10.71	467	22.82	
Unskilled	100.00	1.29	4.83	39.29	48.47	6.12	621	31.54	
Farm	100.00	1.98	2.76	23.32	7.91	64.03	253	12.85	

TABLE 4.13 (Cont.)

PLACE OF BIRTH, DURATION OF RESIDENCE, AND FATHERS' OCCUPATION GROUP	SONS' (GROOMS') OCCUPATION GROUP						SONS' DISTRIBUTION BY FATHERS OCCUPATION GROUP		SONS PROPORTION MOBILE
	Total	Prof., Tech., Management	Clerical, Sales	Skilled, Semi-Skilled	Un-skilled	Farm	N	%	
VETERAN RESIDENTS:									
Total	100.00	5.02	16.60	53.67	13.90	10.81	259	100.00	.564
Prof., Tech., etc.	100.00	16.67	...	(49.58)	(22.22)	(11.11)	18	6.95	
Clerical, Sales	100.00	(8.57)	38.57	42.86	(4.29)	(5.71)	70	27.03	
Skilled, Semi-skilled	100.00	(2.67)	(10.67)	70.67	(12.00)	(4.00)	75	28.96	
Unskilled	100.00	...	(8.45)	53.52	26.76	(11.27)	71	27.41	
Farm	100.00	(8.00)	(8.45)	36.00	(4.00)	44.00	25	9.65	
NEW IMMIGRANTS:									
Total	100.00	3.19	7.62	40.93	30.42	17.84	1,693	100.00	.572
Prof., Tech., etc.	100.00	11.59	21.74	33.33	17.39	15.94	69	4.08	
Clerical, Sales	100.00	6.06	14.07	42.21	23.81	13.85	462	27.29	
Skilled, Semi-skilled	100.00	1.79	5.10	56.89	24.23	11.99	392	23.15	
Unskilled	100.00	1.47	4.42	37.20	51.38	5.52	543	32.07	
Farm	100.00	1.32	2.20	22.03	8.37	66.08	227	13.41	

Source: Israel Central Bureau of Statistics, unpublished marriage data, 1955

dence groups *and* hold sons of skilled and semi-skilled workers. With one exception about seventy percent of the sons of skilled and semi-skilled workers are themselves skilled and semi-skilled, the exception being the Oriental new immigrants; only fifty-seven percent remained skilled or semi-skilled, and twenty-four percent were downward-mobile to unskilled occupations.

4. There is much upward mobility among sons of unskilled workers. Only eleven percent of Israel-born and twelve percent of European veteran settler sons of unskilled workers remained unskilled; but twice as many European new immigrant sons (22%) and somewhat more Oriental veteran settler sons (27%) remained in unskilled occupations. Again, no less than fifty-one percent of the sons of unskilled workers among Oriental new immigrants remained in the unskilled occupational category.

5. In the European-born and Oriental veteran settler groups, the majority of sons of fathers in agriculture *leave* agricultural occupations; but sixty-nine percent of the Israel-born and sixty-six percent of the Oriental new immigrant sons of farmers remain in farm occupations.

6. About three-fourths of the Israel-born and European sons of fathers in clerical, commercial, and sales occupations seek occupations in other categories, the majority in skilled and semi-skilled occupations. By contrast, about two-fifths (39%) of the Oriental veteran settler sons of clerical, sales, and commercial fathers remain in the same category, and the overwhelming majority of those not remaining move to the skilled and semi-skilled category.

The different intergenerational mobility rates by ethnicity and duration-of-residence bear much more detailed and careful study. Thus far, however, they seem to reflect inequality of opportunity for Oriental new immigrants in the occupational sphere: not only do differential rates of access to preferred occupational opportunities by occupational origin operate in their disfavor, but for a *given occupational origin*

there are ethnicity-differential rates of access to occupational
opportunities operating in their disfavor.

VII. SOCIAL MOBILITY AND ECONOMIC GROWTH

It is possible now to turn to the problem of the relationship between social mobility and technological and economic
growth. The typical analysis of this relationship holds that
technological change, economic growth, and consequent
changes in the industrial structure of a nation's economy
generate shifts in the distribution of occupational roles—
whence incumbents of certain newly generated occupational
roles must be recruited from among the available population.[14] In the Western countries this process has operated to
upgrade the occupational structures, i.e., to diminish the
relative numbers of unskilled roles and to increase the relative
numbers of professional, technical, or "white collar" roles,
with consequent changes in prestige structure, style-of-life,
etc. Although high status workers are ordinarily recruited
from high status sectors of the population, the latter population groups are unable to produce or reproduce sufficient
numbers of high status children and new workers to fill both
all the old and the newer high status roles; so that additional
workers in high status employment must be recruited from
lower status elements of the population.

Lipset and Bendix found that patterns of intergenerational
occupational mobility in different Western countries are characterized by some fundamental similarities; and they ascribed
these similarities to the basic similarity in patterns of economic
growth and technological change characteristic of these countries. Sibley suggested a procedure for measuring occupational mobility due to differential fertility separately from
that due to all other factors; and Kahl measured occupational
mobility associated with both differential fertility and with
change in the occupational structure. In all cases both the

14. See, for example, Lipset and Bendix, *op. cit.*

differential fertility and changes in the occupational structure are assumed exogenous to the process of occupational mobility.[15] It has been seen elsewhere that, theoretically at least, it is possible to look at this relationship in an opposite manner: the occupational distribution may well be viewed as the outcome of occupational mobility processes.[16] The case of Israel suggests that there is good practical reason to view the relationship in just this way.

In the first decade of independence the establishment of industries and creation of employment were quite impressive achievements indeed for the new nation; but the pace of establishment of industries has increased markedly in the second decade. Between 1955 (when the labor force statistical series begin) and 1958 the total number of employed males increased by eleven percent while the total number of males employed in manufacturing and industry increased by thirteen percent. But between 1958 and 1961, when the total number of employed males increased by thirteen percent, the number employed in manufacturing and industry increased by no less than twenty-four percent. Though only twenty-four percent of the employed labor force were in industry and manufacturing in 1958, more than half of the 1958-61 additions to the male labor force were absorbed in industry and manufacturing.

Her chronic foreign trade deficit and early financial crises notwithstanding, it is generally well known that Israel has always been blessed with access to many sources of foreign currency in the form of loans, contributions, reparations from West Germany, and successfully-floated bond issues. Thus

15. *Ibid.* Also: J. A. Kahl, *The American Class Structure* (New York: Rinehart & Co., 1957), and Elbridge Sibley, "Some Demographic Clues to Stratification," *American Sociological Review*, VII (1942), reprinted in R. Bendix and S. M. Lipset, (eds.), *Class, Status and Power* (Glencoe: The Free Press, 1953).

16. J. Matras, "Differential Fertility, Intergenerational Occupational Mobility, and Change in Occupational Distribution . . ." *loc. cit.* Also J. Matras, "Social Structural Implications of Technological Changes in Industry in the Chicago Area" in Illinois Institute of Technology Research Institute, *Technological Change Its Impact on Industry in Metropolitan Chicago*, Part 8 (Chicago, 1964).

TABLE 4.14.

EMPLOYED MALES, TOTAL AND EMPLOYED IN MANUFACTURING AND INDUSTRY, 1955-1961; NUM-
BER AND PERCENT CHANGE

	NUMBER EMPLOYED			PERCENT CHANGE		
	Nov. 1955	Average 1958	Average 1961	1955-61	1955-58	1958-61
Total Employed Males	443,000	492,900	556,000	25.5	11.3	12.8
Males Employed in Manufacturing and Industry	104,900	118,600	147,200	40.3	13.1	24.1

Source: Israel Central Bureau of Statistics, *Monthly Statistical Bulletin*, Pt.B, Vol. 13, No. 4, April 1962, Table 9,
p. 395

168

the relatively recent increase in industrial employment cannot be attributed to newly available foreign investment capital.

Indeed, the Government of Israel was for many years subjected to bitter criticism, both domestic and foreign, for insufficient investment in industrial plant. The flow of foreign currency, as well as domestic savings (voluntary or taxation), was, it was asserted, "consumed" or subsidizing consumption, rather than invested in additional capacity. But investment funds alone were for Israel never sufficient for establishment of industries when an industrial working force was absent. In fact many industries were established only to collapse or to be supported by subsidies because productivity was so low that, even with Israeli industrial labor cheaper than its European or American counterpart, the products of Israeli industries could not be marketed competitively, but could be sold only in the protected (very small) domestic market or exchanged in barter agreements with other countries in similar straits. For even if entire plants were imported from abroad, it did not follow that an immigrant population with no experience in industrial employment could be placed at machines and in industrial work settings and thereby converted into an industrial working force.

But the emergence, after almost half a generation of public "investment" in housing, health, and above all in education, of a young industrial work force must be seen as the output of a mobility process. Sons of peddlers, of self-employed artisans, and of petty businessmen of non-industrial cultural origins undergo a socialization process in Israel which includes at least primary education, service in the army, exposure to national consumption patterns, etc., and are able successfully to enter and participate in an industrial work force.

Israel's recent experience suggests that conditions leading to occupational mobility in the population may generate changes in the occupational and industrial structure. The implication for newly developing countries is that investment in human resources, and especially in literacy and in manipulation of verbal and numerical symbols and abstractions, should be prior to direct investment in industrial plant. To be sure, Israel was from the first well-endowed with personnel resources for implementing investments and programs of universal education. But other developing countries and societies might do well to assess their own already-available personnel resources and consider how best to mobilize these for investment directly in population literacy and mobility and, indirectly, in change in the industrial, occupational, and social structures.

5

CHANGES IN THE STRATEGY
OF FAMILY FORMATION

I. INTRODUCTION

SOCIETIES AND social collectivities everywhere have characteristic patterns of courtship, marriage, childbearing, and
family dissolution. Such patterns vary among societies and
social collectivities, and in a given collectivity or society they
may vary over time. The distinctive pattern or distribution of
members of a society over the possible individual courses of
action with respect to marital or family status has been elsewhere called the "social strategy of family formation;" and
it has been noted that *change* in the social strategy of family
formation has implications not only for the rate and structure
of population growth but also for such social structural characteristics as family size, composition of the various age
groups by marital status, and the patterns of inter-group and
inter-collectivity relationships as mediated by intermarriage
between members of distinct subgroups.[1]

In Israel the most important and far-reaching changes in
the strategy of family formation have been of two kinds: 1.
there has been a trend, not spectacular, but readily measurable
and consistent over the years, toward an increasing proportion
of marriages contracted between persons of different geo-
cultural origins, and 2. there has been a trend toward rational-

1. J. Matras, "The Social Strategy of Family Formation: Some
Variations in Time and Space," forthcoming in *Demography*, Vol. 2,
(1965); also J. Matras, "Social Strategies of Family Formation: Some
Comparative Data for Scandinavia, the British Isles, and North America,"
forthcoming in *International Social Science Journal*.

ization or control of childbearing, especially among the Oriental-origin population, but also among traditional or religious sectors of the European-origin population. These two trends, if they continue, will probably be, in the long run, *the* most important factors in the integration of the separate origin groups in a less-heterogenous "Israeli" society.

A fairly detailed statistical record of the frequencies and rates of vital events in the Jewish population of pre-independence Palestine and of post-independence Israel is available. A summary of vital rates is given in Table 5.1. Both the crude birth and gross reproduction rates declined steadily through the two decades, 1920-1940, reaching their lowest point in 1941. Although the crude death rate also declined steadily, the crude rate of natural increase followed the birth rate and declined to a low point in 1941, recovered slightly during and immediately following World War II, and declined in 1948, the year of Israel's War of Independence. With the beginnings of mass immigration in 1948-1949, both the crude birth rate and the crude rate of natural increase rose sharply, reaching peak values in 1951; and both have declined since 1951 to pre-World War II levels in 1962, the last year recorded in Table 5.1.

II. PATTERNS OF MARRIAGE

In an earlier chapter some of the data relating to differences in family status between new immigrants and veteran settlers were reviewed, and in the present section some of the data relating to marriage trends thus far in post-independence Israel are examined briefly. A detailed study of nuptiality in Israel through 1954 has been carried out by K. R. Gabriel, and the present review draws in part upon his results and conclusions.[2]

2. K. R. Gabriel, *Nuptiality and Fertility in Israel* (Jerusalem: Hebrew University Press, 1960, in Hebrew, with English summary).

Israel has the dubious distinction of being one of the few "advanced" countries of the world in which there is no civil marriage or divorce, administrative and legal control over these vital events being still vested in the religious authorities. One consequence, among others, of this situation has been that detailed statistical data on marriages and divorces has been forthcoming only slowly and as a result of a prolonged campaign and negotiation on the part of the Central Bureau of Statistics. Thus while statistics on ages of *all* brides and grooms have been available since 1949, statistics on ages of brides and grooms by previous marital status (especially brides and grooms marrying for the first time) have been available only since 1952, and age statistics for brides and grooms by place of birth have been available only since 1957. On the other hand, religious officials have always distinguished between *Ashkenazic, Sephardic,* and Eastern Jews, and some data on numbers of marriages embodying this distinction are available since 1952. (*"Sephardic"* and "Eastern" Jews together are roughly, but not exactly equivalent to "Oriental" Jews.)

In general, age at marriage has declined slightly in Israel, mostly as a result of the change in ethnic composition of the "marriageable population" and, evidently, of the decline in the number of widows and widowers marrying. Both the Israel-born and the Oriental immigrant components of the adult population single have increased relative to the European-born component; but Israel-born males marry earlier than their Oriental immigrant counterparts while Israel-born females marry later than Oriental immigrant females. Many of the widows and widowers coming in the mass immigration remarried soon after arrival in Israel so that, although the additional widows and widowers keep entering the marriageable population, this component has declined somewhat.

Since 1948 the percent single has increased slightly at ages fifteen to nineteen among both males and females. But at all other ages under fifty-five, the percent single and the percent

TABLE 5.1.

JEWISH POPULATION OF PALESTINE AND ISRAEL: SELECTED VITAL RATES, 1923-1962 (PER 1000 POPULATION)

Year	Crude Birth Rate	Crude Death Rate	Crude Rate of Natural Increase	Gross Reproduction Rate	Infant Mortality Rate	Crude Marriage Rate	Crude Divorce Rate
1923							
1924	35.76	14.08	21.68		121.26	—	—
1925							
1926				1.87			
1927							
1928	34.33	11.63	22.70		94.98		
1929				1.62			
1930				1.50			
1931				1.55			
1932				1.28			
1933	30.32	9.28	21.04	1.29	77.99		
1934				1.32			
1935				1.27		13.59	5.41
1936				1.14			
1937				1.19			
1938	25.74	8.03	17.71	1.09	59.53	12.01	5.31
1939							

174

Year							
1940				1.17			
1941				1.06			
1942				1.20			
1943	26.26	7.51	18.75	1.58	45.93	11.15	2.74
1944				1.67			
1945				1.72			
1946	28.63	6.22	22.41	1.67	31.78	13.02	2.60
1947	30.05	6.17	23.88	—	29.12	12.98	2.20
1948	26.31	6.71	19.60	—	36.26	10.85	1.40
1949	29.95	6.84	23.11	1.66	51.71	13.40	1.68
1950	32.96	6.48	26.48	1.89	46.22	14.54	2.13
1951	32.67	6.41	26.26	1.95	39.20	11.75	1.79
1952	31.57	6.84	24.73	1.93	38.70	11.30	1.68
1953	30.23	6.32	23.91	1.88	35.66	9.56	1.57
1954	27.35	6.42	20.93	1.74	34.12	8.83	1.43
1955	27.22	5.77	21.45	1.77	32.44	8.70	1.32
1956	26.69	6.32	20.37	1.77	35.56	8.44	1.20
1057	26.04	6.18	19.86	1.76	33.36	8.40	1.21
1058	24.05	5.62	18.43	1.65	30.72	8.25	1.20
1959	24.29	5.78	18.51	1.69	27.73	7.89	1.09
1960	23.89	5.53	18.36	1.69	27.23	7.68	1.09
1961	22.68	5.68	17.00		24.24	7.23	0.99
1962	21.95	5.94	16.01		27.47	7.25	1.01

Source: Israel Central Bureau of Statistics, *Statistical Abstract of Israel*, No. 14, 1963.

175

widowed of both sexes have declined, and the percent married and percent divorced have increased.[3] The mean age of brides declined from 25.4 years in 1949 to 24.7 in 1959. The mean age at first marriage was considerably lower for brides in Israel and has declined slightly from 22.8 in 1952 to 22.1 in 1959. The median age at first marriage is considerably lower for females and has remained stable at around 21.0 years in the 1952-1959 period. The mean age at marriage for all grooms declined from 30.6 to 29.3 in the 1949-59 period, and for single grooms it declined from 27.3 to 26.3 in the 1952-59 period. The spread between mean and median age at first marriage has declined somewhat.[4]

European-born single females marry considerably later, on the average, than Israel-born females, but Oriental immigrant single women marry earlier than do women of either of the other groups. Among Israel-born females those of the Oriental communities (Sephardic and Eastern Jews, roughly corresponding to those of Asian-African parentage) marry slightly earlier than those of the *Ashkenazic* communities (roughly, of European parentage or origin). By contrast, Israel-born males of the Oriental communities marry later than those of the *Ashkenazic* communities, Oriental immigrant males marry later than the Israel-born men, and European immigrant males marry later than all the others.[5]

Gabriel estimated nuptiality table probabilities and concluded that the probability of remaining single throughout life in Israel is almost nil for both females and males.[6] Generally the Oriental immigrants marry later in Israel than did Oriental Jews in their communities of origin, and European immigrants marry earlier in Israel than did European Jews between the world wars. Gabriel concluded that for all

3. Israel CBS, *Census of Population 1961 Demographic Characteristics of the Population,* Part I, Table 11, pp. 26-29.
4. CBS, *Statistical Abstracts,* Nos. 3-13. Also J. Matras, "Israel: Absorption of Immigrants, Social Mobility, and Social Change" (Unpublished Ph.D. dissertation, Department of Sociology, University of Chicago, August, 1962).
5. *Ibid.*
6. Gabriel, *op. cit.*

female immigrants, duration of residence in Israel is directly related to age at first marriage, the veteran settlers marrying later than new immigrants, and Israel-born women marrying later than all immigrants. However, the 1957-59 data, which were not available to Gabriel, indicate that European-born women marry later than Israel-born women, and both European and Oriental immigrant men marry later than Israel-born men.

In 1952, marriages between new immigrants and veteran settlers or between new immigrants and Israel-born persons constituted more than a fourth (25.9%) of the total number of marriages contracted in the Jewish population of Israel, and this percentage declined only slightly (to 23.7%) by 1958. Of the 158,000 Jewish marriages contracted in Israel in the period 1949-1959, about one fourth were "mixed" new immigrant-veteran resident marriages. But the percentage of new immigrant-veteran resident marriages is of progressively decreasing interest in that, increasingly, those marrying in Israel are persons who at the cut-off date (1948) were likely to have been small children—whether in Israel or abroad. As duration of residence has been classified in Israeli official statistics (veteran residents—Israel-born or immigrants arriving prior to 1948; new immigrants—those immigrating in 1948 or later) the classification "veteran settler" means that the person marrying was born abroad and immigrated to Israel prior to 1948, say, during World War II at age zero to eight or so, while the classification "new immigrant" means that the person marrying was born abroad and immigrated to Israel in 1948 or after, most likely during the mass immigration of 1948-1951 and at age eight to twelve or so. Even if the distinction is still meaningful in marriage statistics, it is not likely to remain so for very much longer.

On the other hand the distinctions by ethnic or geo-cultural origin have very definitely retained meaning and importance and are likely to continue to do so for some time. Table 5.2 indicates the percentages of *Ashkenazic*-Oriental marriages from 1952 and 1953, the classification based upon the religious grouping (*Ashkenazic, Sephardic,* or Eastern) reported on the marriage certificates, and the percentages of European-Oriental marriages in the 1955-1960 period. The latter classification is based upon country of birth reported on the marriage certificates, with Israel-born of the *Ashkenazic* community included with the European-born and Israel-born of the *Sephardic* and Eastern communities included with those born in Asia and Africa.

It is clear from the table that the percentage of ethnically-mixed marriages increased steadily, if not spectacularly, from 1952 to 1960, climbing from about nine percent in 1952 to 14.4 percent in 1960. It is of interest to note that among the ethnically mixed marriages the marriages of European or *Ashkenazic* males and Oriental females are consistently a substantial majority. By virtually any social or economic index, the European-origin population is "dominant" in Israel, so that the majority of ethnically mixed marriages involve dominant-group males. This pattern contrasts with the more frequent pattern of ethnically-mixed marriages between dominant-group females and minority group males in other countries, and analysis of the differences between Israel and other countries in this respect would surely be of great interest.

The "ethnically mixed" marriages reflect only in part the extent of cross-country-of-birth marriages in Israel. Of 83,686 marriages in the period 1952-1957 for which country-of-birth of both brides and grooms is known, 36,726 of them (about 44%) were marriages between persons of different countries of birth. Of a total of 18,588 Israel-born brides in the 1952-57 period, 9,905 (53%) married foreign-born grooms, and thirty-seven percent of the 13,785 Israel-born grooms married foreign-born brides.[7]

An "index of attraction" has been utilized by the Central Bureau of Statistics[8] to measure the extent to which persons

    7. CBS, *Monthly Statistical Bulletin,* Pt. A., Vol. 10, No. 11, Table 12, p. 576.
    8. *Ibid.,* pp. 558-559, and p. 580. See also J. Matras, "Israel: Absorption of Immigrants . . ." *loc. cit.*

TABLE 5.2.

MARRIAGES IN THE JEWISH POPULATION OF ISRAEL, BY ETHNIC ORIGIN OR COMMUNITY OF ORIGIN OF GROOMS AND BRIDES, 1952-1959

Year	All Marriages, Ethnic or Community of Origin Known	Both Partners Israel-Born, Same Ethnic Origin	Both Partners Foreign-Born Same Ethnic Origin	One Partner Israel-Born, One Foreign-Born, Both Same Ethnic Origin	Mixed Ethnic Origin
NUMBER:					
1952	15,982	885	11,131	1,712	1,254
1953	13,910	968	9,804	1,764	1,374
1955	13,340	1,296	8,467	1,983	1,594
1956	13,617	1,521	8,349	2,034	1,715
1957	14,425	1,735	8,660	2,212	1,818
1958	14,657	1,776	8,651	2,256	1,974
1959	14,437	1,993	8,145	2,297	2,002
1960	14,093	2,243	7,593	2,227	2,030
PERCENT DISTRIBUTION:					
1952	100.0	5.9	73.8	11.3	9.0
1953	100.0	7.0	70.4	12.7	9.9
1955	100.0	9.7	63.5	14.9	11.9
1956	100.0	11.2	61.3	14.9	12.6
1957	100.0	12.0	60.1	15.3	12.6
1958	100.0	12.1	59.0	15.4	13.5
1959	100.0	13.8	56.4	15.9	13.9
1960	100.0	15.9	53.9	15.8	14.4

Source: Israel Central Bureau of Statistics, *Statistical Abstracts of Israel*, Nos. 8-14.

born in a given country tended to marry *within* the same
country-of-origin group in the period 1952-1957. Values of
the index range from zero to 1.0, with the zero-values indicating no tendency toward within-country-of-origin endogamy
and a value of 1.0 indicating complete within-country-of-birth
endogamy. The values of the indexes exhibit some decline
over the six-year period, 1952-1957. However, the value of
the index for Yemen and Aden decreases hardly at all, with
that for French North Africa (Morocco, Tunisia, Algeria)
actually increased, and the value of the index for Israel-born
persons increased. Very much more research on marriage,
and particularly on mixed ethnic and mixed country-of-birth
marriages, is required before much can be said about de-
terminants and consequences of these patterns.

III. FERTILITY AND THE RATIONALIZATION OF CHILDBEARING

The Jewish community in Palestine experienced some-
thing of a baby boom during World War II and, especially,
subsequent to demobilization at the close of the war. But
the biggest baby boom to date took place in the very early
years of Israel's independence, 1950-1953, with the crude
birth rate climbing from 26.31 in 1948, the year of the War
of Independence, to 32.96 in 1950 and declining steadily
since then to 21.95 in 1960 (Table 5.1). The chief reason for
the 1950-53 "boom" was the entrance into the population of
large numbers of Oriental immigrant women characterized
by very much higher fertility than the previously predomi-
nantly European female population of the *Yishuv*, although
fertility rates of both new immigrant European women and
of European veteran settlers rose at the same time, and
the rates for women born in Israel also hit a peak during
the same period.

By 1960 some sixty percent of births in the Jewish population of Israel were to mothers born in Asia and Africa,
compared to twenty-two percent to mothers born in Europe

and America and eighteen percent to mothers born in Israel (Table 5.3). In the 1961 Israel Census, forty-six percent of the Israel-born population under fifteen years of age were reported offspring of immigrant fathers born in Asia or Africa, compared to forty percent children of European immigrants, and fourteen percent children of parents born in Israel.[9]

Within the population of Asian and African origin fertility appears to vary inversely with length of residence in Israel. Gabriel found that the total fertility rate for women of Asian and African origin immigrating prior to 1948 was 5.71 and 4.22 in 1951 and 1954 respectively; whereas for women immigrating in 1948 or later, total fertility rates were 6.50 and 5.96 in 1951 and 1954 respectively.[10] From these and similar data, it has been inferred that with increased duration of residence in Israel there is a growing tendency in the population of Oriental origin toward limitation of family size. The extent to which family limitation is practiced in the various sectors of the population is increasingly recognized as the key variable in fertility trends in Israel. Recently some data directly concerning practice of family limitation have become available, and these are summarized in Table 5.4.[11] The data are from the survey of Jewish maternity cases conducted in 1959-60. The survey was conducted in twenty-three hospitals in Israel (in which some 97% of all births to Jewish mothers took place in 1958) and included *all* women giving birth during a sixty-day period in Tel Aviv-Jaffa, during a forty-two-day period in Jerusalem, and during twelve-day periods in hospitals in all other places. Attention should be directed to an important limitation of the survey:

9. CBS, *Monthly Statistical Bulletin,* Pt. A, Vol. 14, No. 4, April, 1963, Supplement 7: Table 1, p. 217.

10. Gabriel, *op. cit.*

11. These data have been reported in R. Bachi and J. Matras, "Contraception and Induced Abortion Among Jewish Maternity Cases in Israel," *op. cit.;* J. Matras and C. Auerbach, "On Rationalization of Family Formation in Israel," *op. cit.;* and R. Bachi and J. Matras, "Family Size Preferences of Jewish Maternity Cases in Israel," *Milbank Memorial Fund Quarterly,* XLII, Vol. 42, No. 2 (April, 1964).

TABLE 5.3.

BIRTHS IN THE JEWISH POPULATION OF ISRAEL: DISTRIBUTION BY PLACE OF BIRTH OF MOTHER, 1951-1960

Place of Birth of Mother	1951	1953	1954	1955	1956	1957	1958	1959	1960
NUMBER:									
All Places	43,249	44,364	41,046	42,339	43,411	44,817	42,872	44,599	44,981
Asia	13,102	15,311	14,538	14,686	14,347	14,080	13,072	26,870	13,815
Africa	5,399	6,748	6,611	8,026	10,077	11,812	11,708	10,360	13,078
Europe, America	19,771	17,027	14,756	14,011	12,973	12,292	11,220	10,360	10,001
Israel	4,799	5,133	5,048	5,534	5,885	6,607	6,784	7,204	8,087
Unknown	178	145	93	82	129	66	88	165	—
PERCENT DISTRIBUTION:									
All Places	100.0	100.0	100.0	100.0	100.0	100.0	100.0	100.0	100.0
Asia	30.2	34.4	35.5	34.6	33.0	31.3	30.5	60.2	30.6
Africa	12.5	15.3	16.2	19.0	23.3	26.4	27.3	23.2	29.2
Europe, America	45.8	38.4	35.8	33.1	29.9	28.4	26.2	16.2	22.2
Israel	11.1	11.6	12.3	13.1	13.5	14.8	15.8	0.4	18.0
Unknown	0.4	0.3	0.2	0.2	0.3	0.1	0.2		—

Source: *Statistical Abstract of Israel 1962*, No. 3, Part C, Table 26, p. 83.

a survey of maternity cases is necessarily biased with respect to practice of contraception and to induced abortion in the population as a whole. Women practicing contraception are less likely to be included than are those not doing so; and for those practicing contraception, success is inversely related to the likelihood of inclusion in the sample. However, the extent of this bias is directly related to age and order of present birth, and it is felt that for younger women (under 30) and for women with only one or two births the bias is small.

The relationship between geo-cultural origin and duration of residence in Israel to differential fertility in the various sectors of the population born abroad has received considerable attention in analyses of fertility trends in Israel. Questions of change in family size in the different ethnic groups are part of the more general problem of absorption of immigrants and of assimilation of new values and behavior patterns in all other spheres of social and family life. In general, in the twentieth century, Jews in Western countries have been characterized by particularly low fertility, and it has been assumed that, except for the very orthodox Jewish groups, the low fertility rates have been associated with extensive practice of family limitation as well as with late marriage. On the other hand, the Jewish communities in Islamic countries were characterized by relatively early marriage, especially for women, and as far as can be determined, the systematic practice of family limitation was practically unknown in these communities. In the present context it is of particular importance to assess the extent to which immigration to Israel and close contact with the population of Western origin are associated with the introduction of family limitation practices in the Jewish population of Eastern origin.

About forty percent of the women giving birth reported practice of contraception at some time prior to the present birth, and about ten percent reported having had induced abortions. The extent both of the practice of contraception

and of resort to induced abortions varies considerably according to continent of birth and geo-cultural origin. The percentage of women born in Israel and in Europe-America
reporting past practice of contraception (61% and 64% respectively) is more than twice that of women born in Asia-
Africa (25%). While more than a fifth (21%) of the women
born in Europe-America reported having had induced abortions, among women born in Israel and among those born
in Asia-Africa, eleven percent and five percent reported past
induced abortions.

Only about forty percent of all the maternity cases reported ever having considered the number of children they
would like. Of the women born in Israel and Europe-America,
seventy-three percent and sixty-nine percent stated that they
had considered "ideal" family size; but only eighteen percent of the women born in Asia-Africa reported having
considered family size. By contrast, among women of all
origin groups reporting having considered family size preferences, the distributions by *number* of children desired are
remarkably similar. For each geo-cultural origin group, the
modal "choice" is "three" children. Fifty-five percent of the
Israel-born maternity cases, fifty percent of the European-
born women, and forty-four percent of the Asian-African born
women chose "three." In all groups the bulk of the distribution was concentrated in the "two," "three," and "four"
children choices.

In Table 5.4 it is seen that the great majority of maternity
cases born in Israel and in Europe or America completed at
least five years of school—(the "0 years completed" and the
"1-4 years completed" categories are almost empty). Women
born in Israel or in Europe or America who had completed
some post-primary education (9 or more years of school)
were somewhat more likely to have thought of the desired
number of children, but not more likely to have practiced
contraception or to have had an induced abortion than
were those who had had only primary education. But among
women born in Asia and Africa there are very striking dif-

ferences in every family planning characteristic (consideration of desired family size, practice of contraception, induced abortion) between those with no formal schooling and those with some formal education; and among the latter there are notable differences associated with *amount* of education.

More generally, one of the most consistent findings in the studies of fertility of the various sectors of the Jewish population of Israel has been the absence by and large of socio-economic differentiation in fertility patterns among women born in Europe or America and in Israel. Such women classified by characteristics such as education, labor force characteristics, husband's occupation group, family income, duration, type, or place of residence in Israel, etc. exhibit but little differentiation with respect to percent reporting consideration of family size preferences, percent reporting practice of contraception or past induced abortions, or with respect to actual number of live births. By contrast, women born in Asia and Africa are characterized by very notable differentiation and steep gradients with reference to family planning characteristics and to actual number of live births which are associated with virtually every index of socio-economic status, duration-of-residence in Israel, and education. In particular, contrasts between women with no formal education (almost all of whom are illiterate in any language, have had virtually no social contacts outside their primary family groups, etc.) and those with *some* education (and with at least some wider social experience and contacts, past labor force attachments, military service, youth culture experience, etc.) are most striking. And, of course, the Asian-African-born women with no education at all—while not disappearing from the population—will fairly soon "outgrow" the population of fertile women because of "old age."

Accordingly, it may be anticipated that, on the one hand, the fertility of Jewish women born in Asia and Africa will be reduced quite substantially in the near future (barring the entrance into the population of substantial numbers of illiterate new immigrants of child-bearing age) and

TABLE 5.4.

JEWISH MATERNITY CASES IN ISRAEL, 1959-60, BY PLACE OF BIRTH AND NUMBER OF SCHOOL YEARS COMPLETED: PERCENT REPORTING HAVING CONSIDERED NUMBER OF CHILDREN DESIRED, AND NUMBER DESIRED (PERCENT DISTRIBUTION)

	N	% Considered Desired No. Children	NUMBER OF CHILDREN DESIRED					
			Total	1	2	3	4	5+
ALL MATERNITY CASES—TOTAL	7146	39.7	100.0	0.9	31.0	49.9	15.0	3.2
BORN IN ISRAEL—TOTAL	1277	73.2	100.0	0.4	25.2	54.7	16.3	3.4
0 School Years	12	25.0	100.0	—	66.7	—	33.3	—
1-4 School Years	66	22.0	100.0	—	7.7	46.1	38.5	7.7
5-8 School Years	402	60.7	100.0	—	21.2	53.6	19.2	6.0
9-12 School Years	510	79.4	100.0	0.7	24.9	57.8	13.6	5.0
13+ School Years	282	78.6	100.0	0.4	25.0	46.9	21.1	6.6
BORN IN EUROPE, AMERICA—TOTAL	1692	68.9	100.0	1.5	38.8	49.8	7.4	2.5
0 School Years	24	6.3	100.0	—	—	—	—	100.0
1-4 School Years	114	66.7	100.0	8.1	18.9	63.5	9.5	—
5-8 School Years	657	60.9	100.0	2.7	44.9	44.7	6.9	0.8
9-12 School Years	685	73.6	100.0	—	42.3	47.8	7.1	2.8
13+ School Years	212	82.7	100.0	—	29.9	61.1	7.2	1.8
BORN IN ASIA, AFRICA—TOTAL	4177	17.7	100.0	0.5	26.0	43.9	25.4	4.2
0 School Years	1819	3.6	100.0	1.5	9.0	43.3	32.8	13.4
1-4 School Years	711	11.6	100.0	—	29.6	42.0	23.5	4.9
5-8 School Years	1250	31.3	100.0	0.5	25.7	41.3	29.1	3.4
9-12 School Years	367	50.1	100.0	—	30.9	48.9	19.7	0.5
13+ School Years	30	60.7	100.0	—	5.9	52.9	41.2	—

NUMBER OF ACTUAL LIVE BIRTHS (PERCENT DISTRIBUTION)

	% Reporting Contra-ception	% Reporting Induced Abortion	NUMBER OF ACTUAL LIVE BIRTHS						
			Total	1	2	3	4	5	6+
ALL MATERNITY CASES—TOTAL	40.5	9.7	100.0	26.0	25.2	16.8	8.8	6.8	16.4
BORN IN ISRAEL—TOTAL	60.6	11.1	100.0	40.5	30.8	16.7	6.1	2.2	3.7
0 School Years	41.6	18.2	100.0	8.3	25.0	16.7	33.3	—	16.7
1-4 School Years	45.0	14.6	100.0	21.2	9.1	25.7	7.6	19.7	16.7
5-8 School Years	56.8	12.6	100.0	26.4	32.9	21.4	9.7	2.2	7.5
9-12 School Years	64.3	8.5	100.0	45.1	33.5	16.8	3.6	0.4	0.6
13+ School Years	64.2	10.4	100.0	59.0	29.1	8.2	3.9	1.4	0.4
BORN IN EUROPE, AMERICA—TOTAL	64.0	20.8	100.0	31.5	34.1	22.5	6.5	2.1	3.3
0 School Years	50.0	12.5	100.0	4.2	4.2	4.2	8.3	33.3	45.8
1-4 School Years	75.0	29.6	100.0	14.9	29.0	38.6	9.6	6.1	1.8
5-8 School Years	66.0	20.4	100.0	23.0	35.5	28.9	6.1	1.5	5.0
9-12 School Years	64.0	19.4	100.0	43.2	33.2	16.1	6.3	1.2	1.0
13+ School Years	65.6	23.0	100.0	36.4	38.2	17.4	6.2	0.9	0.9
BORN IN ASIA, AFRICA—TOTAL	24.8	4.8	100.0	19.4	19.7	14.7	10.6	10.1	25.5
0 School Years	10.8	2.2	100.0	6.5	10.3	12.6	10.1	14.9	45.6
1-4 School Years	28.2	5.1	100.0	18.9	27.4	18.7	12.5	10.0	12.5
5-8 School Years	35.4	7.9	100.0	30.7	24.8	16.8	12.2	6.8	9.7
9-12 School Years	49.0	2.4	100.0	44.1	35.5	7.6	3.5	0.8	8.5
13+ School Years	62.0	2.4	100.0	33.3	20.0	16.7	16.7	—	13.3

Source: R. Bachi and J. Matras, *Fertility and Contraception—Summary Tables of Surveys of Maternity Cases in Israel,* Jerusalem: mimeographed, 1961, Tables 2, 7, 16, and 28.

on the other hand, the relatively unfavorable conditions under which children of Asian and African-born mothers are brought up—conditions which are associated with the illiteracy and low socio-economic levels of the parents—are likely to see substantial improvement in the near future.

By far the most interesting aspect of changes in patterns of family formation is the rationalization of family formation —the *change* from absence of intervention to control number or spacing of births to family formation characterized by conscious and deliberate intervention—occurring especially among the Oriental immigrant population and among traditional and religious groups in the European immigrant and Israel-born populations. Some of the maternity case data gathered in Jerusalem have been examined elsewhere[12] in a preliminary attempt to describe and analyze these changes, and the main conclusions of this preliminary attempt are reviewed here. In the rest of this section an attempt is made to relate these family formation trends to intergenerational changes in the extent of religious observance discussed in a previous chapter.

Of women in Jerusalem reporting sometime practice of family limitation, about three-fourths (74.8%) reported that their mothers had had four or more live births, and about half the total (49.6%) reported that their mothers had had seven or more live births. Just under half (43.7%) the mothers of the maternity cases reporting sometime practice of contraception were "observant" and another thirty-nine percent were "partially observant."[13] These data, under the assumption that neither the Oriental Jewish communities nor the religious European or Palestinean Jewish communities had been characterized by widespread practice of family limitation in the past, led to the inference that the present generation of young adults (represented in the maternity case data) is characterized by rationalization of family formation.

12. J. Matras and C. Auerbach, *loc. cit.*
13. *Ibid.*

It was possible to document the contention that the women in Jerusalem reporting practice of contraception are —in this generation—accepting and applying the very fact and legitimacy of strategic and tactical consideration in family formation, in radical departure from the previous generation's relegation of family formation to "sacred" realms not amenable to their own manipulation and control. However, *not all* the women are characterized by such a "radical departure," and a major problem is that of the nature of the sorting process: why do some make this "radical departure" while others do not?

The major variables in the process of rationalization of family formation were held to be 1. extent of exposure to small family values and goals, 2. degree of compatibility of small family values and goals with other values and goals, and 3. accessibility to means of implementing these goals.

With reference to the "exposure" variable, two points were made: there are some elements of the Jewish population of Israel still essentially isolated from small family values, or to whom the very idea of conscious intervention to control number or spacing of births is virtually inconceivable. But these population elements include primarily new immigrants from Islamic countries who typically speak and understand no Hebrew, are illiterate in any language, and are more or less cut off from the major facets of social and economic interaction in Israel; and they are quickly disappearing now from the ranks of the fertile population, i.e., are passing the fertile ages and represent a rapidly diminishing proportion of all new family formation.

Besides these elements permanently isolated from small family values, there is a "family cycle effect," consisting of *relative indifference* to questions of family size during the earliest years of marriage; a pattern which is very common among young couples especially in the Oriental community and in the religious and traditional European and Israel-born population groups. Thus there is often a period of no exposure to small family values which ends after the birth of several children leads to the onset of individual-family-scale Malthusian problems.

Even given complete and detailed exposure to small family values and goals, it does not follow that all couples accept these values and goals. In general, the "non-observant" women do all eventually practice family limitation as do the "partially observant" women who are born in Israel or Europe. But the "observant" women of all geo-cultural origins and the "partially observant" of Asian or African birth *may* or *may not* report family limitation practices, depending in part upon whether they accept or reject these goals and values. For those "accepting" the small family values and goals, actual implementation is not always possible. In particular, Oriental couples appear to be characterized by relative absence of husband-wife communication, discussion, and consensus on the topic of family size as well as on other topics.

In the Jerusalem and Tel Aviv-Jaffa maternity case materials from which the intergenerational change data have been taken, both consideration of desired number of children and practice of contraception are reported with rather more frequency than is the case for the countrywide sample. Nevertheless, in Table 5.5 it is seen that the ethnic differentiation is repeated for Jerusalem and Tel Aviv-Jaffa although the differences are less sharp. The same table also indicates the differentiation in family planning behavior by extent of religious observance, and, in almost all cases family planning behavior is inversely related to extent of religious observance.

In both Jerusalem and Tel Aviv the "partially observant" and "non-observant" groups include large proportions of daughters of "observant" mothers.[14] Assuming that—to the extent that family limitation was at all practiced in the previous generation—the inverse relationship between family

14. *Infra.*, Chap. 3; and J. Matras, "Religious Observance and Family Formation in Israel; Some Intergenerational Changes" *op. cit.*

TABLE 5.5.

JEWISH MATERNITY CASES, JERUSALEM AND TEL AVIV, ISRAEL, 1959-60, BY PLACE OF BIRTH AND EXTENT OF RELIGIOUS OBSERVANCE: PERCENT REPORTING HAVING CONSIDERED DESIRED NUMBER OF CHILDREN, AND PERCENT REPORTING PREVIOUS PRACTICE OF CONTRACEPTION.

PLACE OF RESIDENCE AND PLACE OF BIRTH	Total	EXTENT OF RELIGIOUS OBSERVANCE		
		Observant	Partially Observant	Non-observant
I. PERCENT REPORTING HAVING CONSIDERED DESIRED NUMBER OF CHILDREN:				
Jerusalem—Total	34.2	(5.3)	37.4	58.9
Born in Israel	40.5	(5.5)	52.6	55.2
Born in Europe-America	44.0	(8.7)	(42.2)	77.0
Born in Asia-Africa	26.5	(2.8)	30.0	(42.8)
Tel Aviv—Total	54.9	(15.9)	61.0	65.3
Born in Israel	61.0	(20.0)	72.0	69.2
Born in Europe-America	74.8	(37.5)	87.5	80.0
Born in Asia-Africa	35.5	(7.7)	40.0	55.0
II. PERCENT REPORTING PREVIOUS PRACTICE OF CONTRACEPTION:				
Jerusalem—Total	39.2	(8.4)	39.8	71.9
Born in Israel	48.2	(8.3)	54.3	76.2
Born in Europe-America	51.2	(17.4)	58.0	76.8
Born in Asia-Africa	28.5	(2.8)	30.9	57.2
Tel Aviv—Total	66.0	34.1	70.3	82.0
Born in Israel	66.7	(30.0)	56.4	88.3
Born in Europe-America	69.0	(37.5)	68.8	86.5
Born in Asia-Africa	64.4	(34.7)	80.0	74.5

Source: Same as Table 5.4.

planning and extent of religious observance is likely to have
obtained for the mothers' generation as well, the point is
again made that part of the current generation of maternity
cases practicing contraception are in large measure offspring
of mothers *not* practicing contraception and hence characterized by intergenerational change or "rationalization of family formation."

It might seem reasonable to expect that among "partially
observant" and "non-observant" daughters of "observant"
mothers family planning practices would be less frequently
reported than among daughters of "partially-observant" or
"non-observant" mothers, i.e., that there is a first-non-orthodox-
generation effect which would appear among women not
themselves "observant" but daughters of "observant" mothers.
However, this turns out *not* to be the case to any noticeable
degree. In Table 5.6 the percentages reporting ever considering number of children desired and ever practicing contraception among women in each religious observance category by religious observance category of their mothers is
shown. In any given religious observance category the percentages of maternity cases reporting consideration of desired
number of children or practice of contraception do not differ
spectacularly, or even in any noticeably consistent fashion,
by religious observance of the mothers. "Non-observant"
women whose mothers were also "non-observant" do not
appear to be more likely to practice contraception than are
"non-observant" women who *changed* to "non-observance,"
i.e., are daughters of "observant" or "partially observant"
mothers.

Thus, as far as extent of intervention to control number
or spacing of births is concerned, there are immediate effects
of intergenerational changes in the extent of religious observance: the entire sphere of family formation is affected
by the changes in extent of religious observance. It should
be noted that important trends in rationalization of family
formation take place in part independently of change in
the extent of religious observance. This is evident in the per-

TABLE 5.6.

JEWISH MATERNITY CASES, JERUSALEM AND TEL AVIV, ISRAEL, 1959-60, BY EXTENT OF OWN RELIGIOUS OBSERVANCE AND BY EXTENT OF MOTHERS' RELIGIOUS OBSERVANCE: PERCENT REPORTING HAVING CONSIDERED DESIRED NUMBER OF CHILDREN, AND PERCENT REPORTING PREVIOUS PRACTICE OF CONTRACEPTION.

PLACE OF RESIDENCE AND EXTENT OF MOTHERS' RELIGIOUS OBSERVANCE	EXTENT OF OWN RELIGIOUS OBSERVANCE			
	Total	Observant	Partially Observant	Non-observant
I. PERCENT REPORTING HAVING CONSIDERED DESIRED NUMBER OF CHILDREN:				
Jerusalem—All Mothers	34.2	5.3	37.4	58.9
Mothers Observant	23.7	5.0	35.4	(30.0)
Mothers Partially Observant	46.0	0.0	40.8	62.0
Mothers Non-observant	71.1	...	50.0	72.1
Tel Aviv—All Mothers	54.9	(15.9)	61.0	65.3
Mothers Observant	35.5	(17.1)	50.0	(61.3)
Mothers Partially Observant	61.0	(0.0)	68.8	57.1
Mothers Non-observant	72.3	...	(100.0)	72.0
II. PERCENT REPORTING PREVIOUS PRACTICE OF CONTRACEPTION:				
Jerusalem—All Mothers	39.2	(8.4)	39.8	71.9
Mothers Observant	29.9	(8.6)	37.5	75.0
Mothers Partially Observant	52.0	(0.0)	45.0	72.5
Mothers Non-observant	66.0	...	(0.0)	69.3
Tel Aviv—All Mothers	66.0	34.1	70.3	82.0
Mothers Observant	47.0	31.7	62.0	(61.5)
Mothers Partially Observant	79.0	(66.7)	75.8	85.9
Mothers Non-observant	87.5	...	(100.0)	87.0

Source: Same as Table 5.4.

193

centages of "observant" and "partially observant" women
reporting practice of contraception, and some of these trends
have been discussed elsewhere. As far as rationalization
of family formation in Israel is concerned, it is important to
note that it takes place *both* in the form of change in the
extent of religious observance *and* in the apparently increased
legitimacy—within the religious groups and without apparent
changes in "extent of religious observance"—of intervention
in family formation at least to the extent of postponement
of marriage.[15] Thus, on the one hand the religious institutions are increasingly permissive and agreeable to intervention in and rationalization of certain spheres previously held
strictly "sacred;" and on the other hand there is a steady
stream of "defectors" from the religious institutions, collectivities, and subsystems. Both these trends have very far-
reaching implications for virtually every facet of social, economic, and political structure and activities in Israel, and
in particular for patterns and strategies of family formation.

15. J. Matras and C. Auerbach, *op. cit.*

6

SUMMARY AND CONCLUSION

I. THE SPHERES OF SOCIAL CHANGE IN ISRAEL

THIS BOOK has viewed social change in Israel as change in the social structure of the Jewish population of that country. Social structure, in turn, was seen primarily as the set of social roles institutionalized in a society, the pattern of organized and institutionalized relationships between social roles, and the composition of the population by important social roles or key combinations of roles. In this framework the main spheres of social change in Israel treated here were those of 1. population size, composition, and distribution, 2. political organization and its relationship to the population, 3. the occupational structure and its correlates, and 4. marriage and family formation.

It is important to recognize that social change often is and, in the case of Israel could also have been, viewed quite differently. For example, changes in specific institutions (the family, the *kibbutz* or *moshav*, the youth movements, business, and political parties) could have provided foci for a study of social change in Israel. In fact, many such studies of specific social institutions in Israel have been carried out; and often their detail and depth exceed by far the levels which were, or could have been, attempted in the global and more general treatment undertaken in this small volume.

Alternatively, analysis of changes in attitudes or values or in behavior, child-rearing, courtship, or participation in organizations might have been viewed as the most important facets of social change. Finally, change in social issues, in

195

social problems, or in types of social disorganization might have been treated as the central concerns of a study of social change.

While the particular choice of spheres of social change is not intended to imply rejection of alternative approaches to analysis of social change in general or of social change in Israel in particular, neither is it an arbitrary choice. Rather, it reflects what may be called an ecological perspective with respect to social structure and social organization. The ecological perspective holds that social structure is intimately related to population size, composition, and growth characteristics, as well as to the technology to which it has access and to the geographical and physical environment in which it must seek its sustenance. Moreover, the composition of a population by social roles and key combinations of social roles is itself a fundamental facet of social structure. Thus at every juncture an effort has been made to relate social roles and social institutions to population and population composition.

Sociology and related disciplines are *scientific* disciplines only to the extent that their propositions have reference to, and are verifiable in terms of, data generated by events and phenomena in the real world; and to the extent that empirical representations and verifications are cast in a manner permitting their replication by independent investigators. In the social sciences as well as in other scientific disciplines, symbolic representation of events or phenomena in the real world have tended to be mathematical or statistical in form, thus permitting summary, description, manipulation, and analysis by more or less standard mathematical techniques. Accordingly, we have sought statistical representations of social structure and of change in social structure wherever possible. The ecological perspective is congenial to a scientific (in the sense above) approach to social structure both in that it deals with identifiable and circumscribed populations and because of its use, typically, of exhaustive and mutually exclusive descriptive categories in their analysis. Accordingly, the data collection and analysis procedures and techniques so familiar in demography and population studies may be mobilized and applied to the study of social structure and of change in social structure.

Generally social change in Israel was viewed with reference to the social structure of the *Yishuv*, the Jewish community in pre-independence Palestine, in so far as inferences could be drawn about that community's social structure. But in certain instances relationships were sought between change in Israel and social situations obtaining in the Jewish communities outside Palestine and Israel, the communities from which the present population of Israel or its immediate forebears emigrated. But problems both of specification of the social structure of the *Yishuv* and of the Jewish communities abroad, and of tracing the process by which certain social structural elements were selected, carried over, and preserved in Israel while others vanished, operated at many points to render the analysis incomplete, inadequate, or unsatisfactory.

The analysis by S. N. Eisenstadt of the change in social structure of the Jewish community in Palestine which accompanied achievement of independence and the mass immigration of Jews from both Europe and the Islamic countries of Asia, North Africa, and the Middle East falls short both of being an adequate sociological description of the *Yishuv* and of describing adequately the ensuing changes in social structure. The key to this inadequacy is Eisenstadt's failure to specify, and indeed his apparent lack of interest in or awareness of, the relationship between the social structure of the organized Zionist political and economic institutions and the general population. This in turn derives from the systematic neglect of the relationship between theoretical analysis and assertions and the empirical phenomena and events which such theory purports to describe, the neglect of relevant empirical data where they have existed, and the failure to seek new data which, in addition to bearing upon the problems being treated, could be meaningfully related to their population base and could have permitted independent replication and verification.

The notion that economic differentiation in the *Yishuv* was independent of social prestige, of political power, of country of origin and duration of residence in Palestine, and that successive waves of immigrants to the *Yishuv* were promptly absorbed into all social, economic, and political spheres of the organized Jewish community without segregation or discrimination seems consistent enough with Zionist ideology and with assertions emanating prior to independence from the organized Palestinean Jewish political institutions. But this notion is nowhere supported by any systematic data. To be sure neither is it contradicted by any systematic data; but the post-independence data suggesting ethnic-origin and period-of-immigration social differentiation and residential and economic segregation could as readily and as reasonably be interpreted as reflecting continuation of a pre-statehood pattern rather than as they have been interpreted: as reflecting very strong and abrupt changes. The kinds of data which might bear upon characterization of the relationship of the political structure of the *Yishuv* to the general population were suggested in Chapter 3; and types of data essential for more adequate characterization of other facets of the social structure of the *Yishuv* have been suggested or hinted in the other chapters. Unfortunately, in almost every case such data seem not readily available nor, indeed, are they likely to become available in the future.

Finally, it is very important to stress the fact that discussion here has been limited to the *Jewish* population of Israel. As of the 1961 Census of Population, the non-Jewish population of Israel included no less than 247,000 residents, comprising some 11.3 percent of the total population. The non-Jewish population, and the Moslem population in particular, have recently been characterized by what are perhaps the most spectacular rates of natural increase ever recorded.

The most important development in the non-Jewish pop-

ulation of Israel since independence has been the progress in
the direction of universal literacy. The present school-age
generation in the non-Jewish population of Israel represents
the very first Arabic-speaking population cohort characterized
by almost universal literacy. The implications and consequences of these changes have barely been considered, much
less plotted in detail. But socio-economic developments in
the non-Jewish population of Israel will surely be of enormous interest both inside and outside of Israel. That these
trends are not considered here in any detail is not at all to
minimize their importance; on the contrary, changes characterizing the non-Jewish population of Israel are of crucial
importance for the Jewish population as well, and they deserve
full and detailed study and analysis.

Unfortunately, the non-Jewish population of Israel, mostly
Moslem and Christian Arabs, is too often compared to the
Arab populations of neighboring countries. In such comparisons the non-Jewish population is inevitably seen to be
enjoying high levels of health, welfare, education, and consumption. Comparisons of the non-Jewish population with the
Jewish population of Israel have, for the most part, been
left to writers with an anti-Israel bias. The latter inevitably
conclude from their comparisons that the non-Jewish minority
comprises a population of "second class citizens" pure and
simple. In fact the non-Jewish minority does not comprise an
exploited or "second class citizen" population; but neither
is it integrated residentially or in the social, economic, and
cultural institutions of Israel.

The reasons for the institutional segregation of the Arabic-
speaking minorities lie not only in the often-cited political
ambivalence and ambiguities characterizing these communities and their individual members and families; but, also,
they would appear to include the institutionalized linguistic
differences (e.g., in official recognition of Arabic as the language of instruction, public business, etc.; whereas even for
Arabic-speaking Jewish immigrant groups Hebrew is the
language of instruction and the language of the younger gen-

eration); the very deep ties to the land, to agriculture, and to agrarian social institutions; and to rigidities of the traditional extended family system. It seems clear that changes are taking place in some, if not all, of these areas, but the investigation and analysis of these changes is beyond the scope and competence of the present volume.

II. SOCIAL CHANGE IN ISRAEL

The most obvious social change occurring in Israel has been the spectacular growth of the Jewish population. This growth was accompanied by even more spectacular changes in the ethnic or geo-cultural composition of the population and by expansion of settlement to areas of the country not previously inhabited or settled by Jews. Many new settlements and towns arose composed almost exclusively of new immigrants; and two of the largest cities, Tel Aviv-Jaffa and Haifa, have taken on a metropolitan character. The population growth and compositional changes have affected virtually every facet of social structure in Israel.

The political structure of Israel may be undergoing shifts in the basis of popular support for the respective political parties. Three factors were noted in this process: in the first place, the transfer of functions of government from the voluntary organizations of the *Yishuv* to the ministries and bureaus of the government of Israel created social distances between officials and political leaders and the rank-and-file Zionists. In the second place, the immigration of large numbers of individuals and groups oriented principally to immediate personal and family, rather than to national, concerns forced political parties to shift attention to such interests and concerns. Finally, the sector of the population presumably most inclined to "vote" its ideologies, *viz.*, the orthodox religious sector, was seen both to be obviously *not* systematically voting the "religious ticket" and to be affected by secularization and diminishing adherence to religious prescriptions and traditions. The secularization trend, of great interest in itself, was seen to be occurring principally in the Oriental-origin population and associated positively with education, with other correlates of increasing socio-economic, status, and with increasing duration of residence in Israel.

The reaction of the political parties to the shift in the basis of electoral support has probably been both to temper ideological rigidities and to broaden their organizational bases. Again it is important to stress the absence, thus far, of systematic data concerning the political structure of Israel: data concerning the political roles and institutions, differential participation and recruitment to political roles, and population bases of political support for the various parties have simply not been developed; and such data as exist— e.g., the areal data on election returns—have not yet been sufficiently analyzed and exploited. But if this tentative analysis is correct, there are certain implications both for Israel and for other "emerging societies." In a politically independent society political movements and institutions must not only formulate proposals concerning public policy, but if they achieve power, they must also carry them, or *some* policy, out. This process is a far cry from exerting pressure upon a "foreign" governing institution or establishment; and in particular the governing process requires different talents, different experience, different bases of political support than does revolution or the process of "lobbying" or "protest" or exertion of pressure. Moreover, while "protest" may generate varying degrees of support, it is as likely to encounter indifference among non-supporters as it is to encounter opposition. But government and administration inevitably generate individual and often organized non-compliance and opposition. Upon the manner and effectiveness with which the governing body mobilizes support and resources depends its positive success in promoting the goals of the society; and upon the manner in which the governing body handles individual and organized opposition depends the relationship between the governors and the governed. In the newly-independent countries the political organizations in the forefront of independence movements must seek to broaden the base of their support and of human resources which may be mobilized to effect or move toward the promised reforms, improvements and progress. Failure to do so dooms such reform and improvement programs to failure and forces incumbents in political office to seek to retain their power by suppression of opposition and strengthening and consolidation of their narrow bases of support. But the shift from ideological issues to broader-based social, economic, or sectional "interests" as foci of political support operates positively to broaden the bases of political support and participation.

The changes in the occupational sphere and its correlates have involved chiefly increasing levels of literacy among those sectors of the population previously characterized by low literacy levels and the emergence of an industrial work force. The latter was seen to be associated with mobility processes in which sons of white collar and independent small-scale entrepreneurs, as well as sons of unskilled persons, are more likely to become skilled or semi-skilled employees than any other category of worker. This mobility process, including socialization, at least primary education, and military service in Israel, generated shifts in the occupational structure which, in turn, have been the key factor in changing the industrial structure of the economy.

In pre-independence Palestine, "Back to the Soil" was a characteristic Zionist slogan, and there were many solid political and economic justifications for such an ideology. But in post-independence Israel it was immediately clear that the future welfare of any sizable population lay in rapid industrialization of the country and of the population of former shopkeepers, bureaucrats, petty tradesmen, and professionals. The post-independence channeling of new immigrant families to new cooperative agricultural villages was primarily a scheme for absorption of immigrants with few if any in-

dustrial labor market skills rather than a scheme for en-
larging the agricultural sector. Large-scale investment in
industry in Israel had to await the increments to the industrial working force generated by the schools and the military
services.

If this analysis is correct, there are, again, some broader
implications both for Israel and for other developing societies. The most important and first area of investment and
development must be in human resources. Literacy, famili-
arity with the historical and cultural symbols of the society,
ease of manipulation of symbols and abstractions, and fa-
miliarity with approaches to rational problem-solving are the
outputs of universal primary education; and their absence
dooms any society to relative economic stagnation regardless of the investment of resources into other areas and
directions of development.

Finally, the analysis of marriage indicated that a significant and consistently increasing proportion of Jewish marriages in Israel are cross-ethnic-group marriages, a trend
which in the long run will operate to overcome the structural disadvantage of the Oriental population in Israel. Child-
bearing is increasingly characterized by rational considerations and by efforts to control numbers and spacing of
children.

There is good reason to suppose that the increasing number of cross-ethnic marriages is associated with increasing
education. Though rigid ethnic-group endogamy has been
a characteristic only of the least-educated groups, on the
one hand, and of the most rigidly orthodox religious groups,
on the other hand, marriage within broad continent-of-birth
or geo-cultural categories has been and remains the rule
rather than the exception. The latter is a consequence of
socio-economic level patterns of propinquity rather than
strictly ethnic, country-of-origin, or linguistic endogamy.

The rationalization of family formation is, of course, not
new to Jews of European origin. But the extension and increasing acceptance of family limitation practices among

Oriental Jews and among religious or partially-observant Jews is properly viewed as an index—perhaps the most extreme possible index—of more general tendencies towards acceptance and institutionalization of means-ends thinking and behavior on both individual and family levels. Extension of efforts to control fertility is related to increased education, economic activity of women outside the home, and increased duration of residence in Israel; and presumably other types of rationalization are likewise related to these factors. Implications of these trends for institutions outside the family have yet to be considered and analyzed.

Two implications of the investigations of rationalization of family formation in Israel seem clear: that *some* education—or more correctly, literacy and some ability to deal with symbols and abstractions—is the *sine qua non* of consideration of family size and evolvement of family size preferences, to say nothing of action toward realizing such preferences or limits; and development of small family values and readiness to accept or try family limitation practices late in marriage is, for the most part, irrelevant to ultimate family size. Only couples having an early start on rationalization of family formation can really control family size effectively. Those beginning late in marriage may participate in some reduction of the birth rate of the population as a whole, but they do not successfully control their own family size.

III. FROM "MARGINAL" TO "NON-MARGINAL" SOCIETY

In the first chapter the question of the structure of "marginal" societies or collectivities was raised; and it was suggested that perhaps certain types of roles or institutions may be peculiar to or exhibit dominance in "marginal" societies while others are dominant in "non-marginal" societies. In particular, it was suggested that a collectivity's emergence from "marginal" to "non-marginal" status may entail increasing emphasis upon or importance of certain roles and institutions.

Some, but not all, of the data and discussion of the previous chapters bear upon this point. The *Yishuv*, it was suggested, was a "marginal" community in many of the same respects as were Jewish communities abroad. Jewish political and communal institutions in pre-independence Palestine had much the same functions and much the same relationships to the non-Jewish governing bodies as did their counterparts in the Jewish communities abroad. The Jewish community of pre-independence Palestine was an urban community to only a slightly lesser extent than were Jewish communities elsewhere, though relatively more Jews *were* engaged in manual occupations in the *Yishuv* than was the case abroad. Independence, the exodus of the majority of the Arab population of Palestine, and the mass immigration of additional Jews both generated new political and economic roles and reshuffled both the veteran settler population of Palestine and the new immigrant Jewish population of Israel over the previous set of social roles.

The shift from voluntary organization to bureaucratic administration and rule, the secularization trends, and the shift of the bases of popular electoral support for the various political parties would appear to be manifestations of movement of the society from "marginal" to "non-marginal" or, from "dependent" to "independent" status. The data showing intergenerational mobility in the direction away from non-manual occupations and "intellectual" pursuits, and the emergence of an industrial working force replacing, as it were, the merchants, middlemen, clerks, and liberal-professionals of Jewish collectivities outside Israel and Palestine also lend themselves to such an interpretation. Both types of change may be said to imply or symbolize diminishing involvement of the collectivity with manipulation of ideas, ideals, and ideologies, and increasing involvement with manipulation of the physical and material world.

The hypothesis is far from being confirmed in any satisfactory manner; but possibly it could be applied and tested
in other socio-historical situations wherein societies emerge
from political and economic dependence and subordination
to independent status. The hypothesis would be confirmed
to the extent that such societies be characterized by changing social structure in the direction of diffusion and redistri-
bution of the population over a *wider range* of social roles
than was the case under dependent or "marginal" status.
The hypothesis would be disproved to the extent that such
societies be characterized by increasing role-specialization
or concentration of the population over a smaller set or
narrower range of social roles than was the case under dependent or "marginal" status. The hypothesis would likewise
be disproved for Israel if that country should become,
eventually, very highly specialized and concentrated in
some narrow set of social, economic and political roles.

IV. CONCLUDING REMARKS

An attempt has been made in these pages to plot, if only
in broad outline, the major axes, lines, and directions of
change in the social structure of Israel. Wherever possible we
have drawn upon empirical data to form statistical representations of social structure and of social change; and where
such data have not been available, we have decried their absence and protested our distress. But this emphasis upon use
of empirical materials must not be misconstrued to read
that all social scientists studying in or about Israel should
turn immediately to collection of data. It is worth remark-
ing that no data were collected specifically for the purposes
of this present work. Rather, all the data had either been
previously published or were freely available from Israel's
Central Bureau of Statistics or from the Hebrew University
in Jerusalem. Much research initiative which falls by the
wayside for "lack of data," because of absence of resources

for collection of new data or because of entanglement in vast data-collection and data-analysis operations, might well be saved and promoted by exploitation of data already collected and fairly readily available. If the present work is in any way suggestive in this respect, it will have served a useful purpose.

If societies be viewed as human aggregates organized for collective adaptation to their environments, then surely the historically relevant environments of Jewish societies and collectivities the world over must be seen as human rather than geographic or physiographic environments. But human environments, perhaps not so unlike physiographic environments, could be characterized by greater or lesser degrees of hospitality, or by greater or lesser hostility. Accordingly, for Jewish societies and social collectivities, the strategies of survival and adaptation were inevitably cultural, intellectual, political, religious, and ideological rather than economic and technological.

But Israel is a Land as well as a people and a society; and, as in ancient times, modern Israel's social strategy of survival and adaptation must be economic and technological; for there are no host societies, no imperial powers to see to Israel's physical and material survival. Yet Israel has still a human environment—neighboring societies in her region, in the world community, and in her own history. The evolvement of social patterns embodying both economic and technological *and* cultural and intellectual strategies of survival and adaptation would appear to be both Israel's challenge and her opportunity.

INDEX